on or
date below.

AS Psychology
UNIT 2
2ND EDITION

AQA

Specification

A

Module 2: Physiological Psychology and Individual Differences

044014

Philip Allan Updates
Market Place
Deddington
Oxfordshire
OX15 0SE

tel: 01869 338652
fax: 01869 337590
e-mail: sales@philipallan.co.uk
www.philipallan.co.uk

ISBN 0 86003 883 1

This Guide has been written specifically to support students preparing for the AQA Specification A AS Psychology Unit 2 examination. The content has been neither approved nor endorsed by AQA and remains the sole responsibility of the author.

Printed by Raithby, Lawrence & Co Ltd, Leicester

Contents

Introduction

■ ■ ■

Content Guidance

■ ■ ■

Questions and Answers

Introduction

About this guide

This is a guide to Unit 2 of AQA(A) AS Psychology, which examines the content of **Module 2: Physiological Psychology and Individual Differences**. This guide is intended as a revision *aid*, rather than a textbook or revision guide. Therefore, the emphasis is on *how* the specification content is examined and on showing you how different levels of answer to sample questions will be assessed.

The two compulsory sections of AQA(A) Physiological Psychology and Individual Differences are covered, and for each of these we take you through the following:
- the specification content for each topic. This is fully explained so that you know exactly what you might be asked to demonstrate in an examination.
- appropriate content relevant to those topics. This gives you a minimal coverage of each topic area. This is not intended as the *only* appropriate content for a given topic area, but does give you an idea of how you might present your answer to a question set on this particular aspect of the specification.
- a set of definitions of key terms for each section, vital for those 'What is meant by?' questions. Each of these has been constructed to be succinct but informative and therefore appropriate for such questions.
- *four* sample questions in the style of AQA(A) AS examination questions, together with full explanations of their requirements. These questions demonstrate the typical format of AQA(A) AS questions, as well as the appropriate breakdown of marks between AO1 and AO2 skills (see page 5).
- a typical 'grade B/C' student response to each of these questions, together with examiner comments showing where the marks have been gained and lost.
- a 'grade A' response to each of these questions, showing how they might have been answered by a very good student.

How to use this guide

This book is not intended as a set of model answers to examination questions, nor as an account of the *right* material to include should you be asked to display this very same knowledge. It is intended to give you an idea of the way that your examination will be structured and how you might improve your own examination performance.

It is suggested that you read through the relevant section in Content Guidance before attempting a question from the Question and Answer section, and only read the specimen answers after you have tackled the question yourself.

The examination: AO1 and AO2 questions

Unit 2 is assessed in a *1 hour* examination. Your examination paper will comprise *four questions*, two of which are on Physiological Psychology and two on Individual Differences. You are required to select *one* on Physiological Psychology and *one* on Individual Differences.

Each question is worth *30 marks*. Within each question, there will be *three parts*. The *last part* is always the **AO1 + AO2** part of the assessment, and the preceding parts are purely **AO1**. The **AO1** question parts test your *knowledge* and *understanding* skills, while **AO2** tests your skills of *analysis* and *evaluation*.

Questions

The following are examples of the types of question that are used to assess AO1 and AO2.

AO1 questions

What is meant by the terms 'stressor', 'cardiovascular disorders' and 'stress management'? *(2+2+2 marks)*

Describe two differences between anorexia nervosa and bulimia nervosa.
(3+3 marks)

Describe the aims/procedures/findings/conclusions* of one study of the impact of workplace stressors. *(6 marks)*

[*any combination of two of these aspects of the study]

Outline two physical approaches to the reduction of stress. *(3+3 marks)*

Describe one explanation of anorexia nervosa. *(6 marks)*

Give two criticisms of the explanation you have given above. *(3+3 marks)*

AO1 + AO2 questions

Consider how attempts to define abnormality might be influenced by cultural differences. *(18 marks)*

Outline and *Evaluate* the physical approach to stress management. *(18 marks)*

'All cultures experience stress, but the sources of the stress, and even the ways in which people deal with it, may differ from culture to culture.'
To what extent have cultural differences been shown to modify the effects of stressors? *(18 marks)*

Effective exam performance

- *Read the questions carefully*, as marks are only available for the specific require-ments of the question set. Miss those out and you lose marks; include something irrelevant and you have wasted valuable time.

- Remember that *each mark* is equivalent to approximately *1 minute* of thinking and writing, so it is vital to use this time wisely, neither extending it nor skimping on it.

- *Make a brief plan* before answering the question. This can be in your head or on paper, but you must know where you are going and how long it will take you to get there. *Time management is absolutely vital*.

- Sometimes questions ask you to *outline* something. You need to practise doing this as the skill of précis is not as easy as it looks.

- *Be aware of the difference between AO1 and AO2 questions*. AO2 questions are not just an opportunity for more descriptive content. You must *engage with the question topic* in the required way.

- In AO1 questions, the emphasis is on the *amount* of relevant material presented (e.g. 'limited' or 'basic'), the amount of *detail* given (e.g. 'lacking detail') and the *accuracy* of the material (e.g. 'muddled').

- For the AO2 component of AO1 + AO2 question parts, the emphasis is on the *amount* and *level* of the critical commentary (e.g. 'superficial'), its *thoroughness* (e.g. 'reasonably thorough') and how *effectively* it has been used (e.g. 'highly effective').

How are the marks awarded?

Mark allocations for AO1 2-mark questions

'What is meant by the terms 'stressor', 'cardiovascular disorders' and 'stress man-agement'?'   *(2+2+2 marks)*

Marks	Criteria
2 marks	Accurate and detailed
1 mark	Basic, lacking detail, muddled or flawed
0 marks	Inappropriate or incorrect

Mark allocations for AO1 3- and 6-mark questions

'Outline two physical approaches to the reduction of stress.'   *(3+3 marks)*

'Describe one explanation of anorexia nervosa.'   *(6 marks)*

3-mark questions	6-mark questions	Criteria
3 marks	6–5 marks	Accurate and detailed
2 marks	4–3 marks	Limited, generally accurate but less detailed
1 mark	2–1 marks	Basic, lacking in detail, muddled or flawed
0 marks	0 marks	Inaccurate or irrelevant

Mark allocations for AO2

Certain questions are AO1 + AO2. They are awarded 18 marks: 6 marks AO1 (assessed using the criteria above) and 12 marks AO2, assessed according to the criteria below. The heading '**commentary**' applies to the specific AO2 requirement of the question (e.g. 'evaluate' or 'to what extent?').

Marks	Commentary	Analysis	Use of material
12–11	Informed	Reasonably thorough	Effective
10–9	Reasonable	Slightly limited	Effective
8–7	Reasonable	Limited	Reasonably effective
6–5	Basic	Limited	Reasonably effective
4–3	Superficial	Rudimentary	Minimal interpretation
2–1	Just discernible	Weak and muddled	Mainly irrelevant
0	Wholly irrelevant	Wholly irrelevant	Wholly irrelevant

Content
Guidance

In this section, content guidance is offered on the topics of stress (Physiological Psychology) and abnormality (Individual Differences).

Each topic begins with an outline and explanation of the AQA Specification A requirement for this part of the module. This is followed by a more detailed look at the theories and studies that make up the module content.

Knowledge of appropriate theories and studies is essential for the AS examination. It is also important to be able to assess the value of these theories and studies, and this is done in regular 'Evaluation' features.

At the end of each topic, definitions are provided for key terms — those terms that you might be asked to define in an examination.

Names and publication dates have been given when referring to research studies. The full references for these studies should be available in textbooks should the reader wish to research the topic further.

Physiological psychology: stress

Stress as a bodily response

Specification content

The body's response to stressors, including the general adaptation syndrome (Selye). Research into the relationship between stress and physical illness, including cardio-vascular disorders, and the effects of stress on the immune system.

Here you are expected to know how the body responds to stressors, for example the role of the **autonomic system** and the **pituitary gland**. You are specifically required (note the use of the term 'including') to know about Selye's **general adaptation syndrome** and should be able to summarise its three stages of stress response.

The use of the term 'research' should alert you to the possibility of questions relating to *studies* of the relationship between stress and illness. These might ask specifically for research studies that have explored the relationship between stress and **cardio-vascular disorders** and the **effects of stress on the immune system**. When revising research studies in these areas, make sure you can summarise the *aims*, *procedures*, *findings* and *conclusions* of each study.

How does the body respond to stressors?

The hypothalamic–pituitary link

The hypothalamus controls the pituitary gland, which in turn controls the adrenal cortex (part of the adrenal gland). The pituitary releases adrenocorticotrophic hormone (ACTH) into the bloodstream. This travels to the adrenal cortex and stimulates the release of corticosteroids; these have a range of effects on different parts of the body, which are significant in a response to stress.

The role of the autonomic nervous system (ANS)

The ANS controls the adrenal medulla. Stimulation by the sympathetic division of the ANS causes the adrenal medulla to release adrenaline and noradrenaline into the bloodstream. These stimulate heart rate and blood pressure and mobilise energy resources. As a result, oxygen is mobilised to the muscles as part of the 'fight or flight' response to stress.

General adaptation syndrome (GAS)

Selye (1956) proposed a sequence of stages as a way of explaining how the body reacts to stressful situations. The model also explains how prolonged exposure to stress can lead to the development of stress-related illnesses, such as gastric ulcers.

There are three stages in GAS:

- the **alarm** stage, when the sympathetic branch of the ANS is activated. This increases heart rate and blood pressure and stimulates the release of hormones that maintain and increase sympathetic activity
- the **resistance** stage, where the body attempts to cope with the stressor by maintaining the same level of arousal
- the **exhaustion** stage, where the body's resources and defence against the stressor become exhausted. At this stage, stress-related conditions such as ulcers and raised blood pressure can develop

Evaluation

+ GAS has been useful in explaining the relationship between exposure to stressors and physical illness. Many illnesses, such as depression, ulcers and anxiety, can be explained in terms of the body's prolonged exposure to a perceived threatening stressor.

− Selye's experimental work was restricted to non-human animals and emphasised the importance of physical stressors. It fails to acknowledge the importance of *psychological* aspects of stress in humans (such as their cognitive appraisal of a situation).

− Although many people do develop stress-related disorders, there are considerable differences in the *types* of disorder that they experience as a result of their prolonged exposure to stress. The same bodily processes are involved, but the way in which these lead to specific disorders must involve other physical or psychological processes.

Stress and the cardiovascular system

As part of the body's stress response, stored carbohydrates and fats are released into the bloodstream. When the stressful situation passes, these are usually reabsorbed. If the stress is prolonged, however, reabsorption cannot cope, and these substances stay in the bloodstream where they fur up the cardiovascular system, leading to raised blood pressure and atherosclerosis.

The body's stress response also causes an increase in heart rate, with blood being pumped around the body at a faster rate and at higher pressure. This increased mechanical pressure can lead to increased damage of the blood vessels. The resulting scarring of blood vessels acts as a collection point for circulating fatty acids and glucose, and this can lead to the formation of plaques that eventually block the blood vessels (the process of atherosclerosis).

Research evidence

Russek (1962)

The aim of Russek's study was to see whether individuals exposed to high levels of occupational stress showed a higher prevalence of coronary heart disease than those exposed to lower levels of occupational stress.

Russek sent questionnaires to four groups of age-matched medical professionals. Two of these groups (GPs and anaesthetists) were judged to be in high-stress areas of medical practice. The other two (pathologists and dermatologists) were judged to be in low-stress levels of medical practice. The questionnaires measured family diet and incidence of coronary heart disease in the sample.

Results from the questionnaires showed that the high-stress groups were more prone to coronary heart disease than the low-stress groups. The prevalence of coronary heart disease was greatest among GPs (11.9% of the sample) and lowest among dermatologists (3.2% of the sample).

This study confirms the relationship between stress associated with job responsibility and the development of coronary heart disease. Russek further concluded that such stress appeared far more significant in the development of heart disease than hereditary factors or a high-fat diet.

Stress and the immune system

The immune system protects the body from infection by harmful viruses and bacteria and helps in the repair of tissue damage. Short-term stress leads to the suppression of the immune system (through the action of corticosteroids), as all resources are diverted to deal with the stressful situation. Corticosteroids stop the production of lymphocytes (white blood cells) which destroy infectious agents. Studies show that colds and other latent infections manifest themselves on weekends after busy and stressful work weeks. Short-term suppression of the immune system is not dangerous, as it is self-regulating and so will recover from suppression when the stressful situation has passed.

Long-term suppression of immune function can leave the body vulnerable to infection and disease. The acute effects of psychological stressors can affect asthma, a disease that involves both external and internal factors. Studies have shown that some children with chronic asthma improve considerably when away from their parents. The changes might be due to the removal of a stressful interaction between the asthmatic child and his/her parents.

Research evidence
Kiecolt-Glaser et al. (1987)

The aim of Kiecolt-Glaser et al.'s study was to see whether people who were exposed to prolonged stress (long-term carers of Alzheimer's disease patients) would also have lowered immune function, which would in turn make them more vulnerable to illness.

Kiecolt-Glaser et al. compared an Alzheimer's carers group with an age-matched control group. They measured the activity of their immune system from blood samples as well as measuring various aspects of psychological functioning, such as life satisfaction and depression scores. They also tested the recuperative functions of each participant by measuring how long it took their body tissue to recover from a minor arm wound.

Results showed that the Alzheimer's carers had lower levels of life satisfaction and higher levels of depression, and their body tissue took significantly longer to heal following a wound. This group also showed significant immunosuppression, with lower levels of helper T lymphocytes and natural killer (NK) cells.

The conclusion was that carers of Alzheimer's patients are more depressed and have a poorer immune function. However, despite this, there were no significant differences in overall health levels between the two groups.

> **Evaluation**
>
> + These findings have important implications for treating people with infections, particularly in situations where they are recovering from surgery. It is important to reduce stress as far as possible in such patients and so speed their recovery.

Sources of stress

Specification content

Research into sources of stress, including life changes (e.g. Holmes and Rahe), and workplace stressors (e.g. work overload, role ambiguity). Individual differences in modifying the effects of stressors, including the role played by personality (e.g. Friedman and Rosenman), culture and gender.

Here you are expected to know about the **sources of stress**. You are specifically required to know **research studies** into the role of **life changes** and **workplace stressors** as sources of stress. The use of 'e.g.' instead of 'including' means you cannot be asked specifically about the work of Holmes and Rahe, or about work overload or role ambiguity. These are merely *examples* to help you decide what is an appropriate way to answer a question in this area. Make sure you can offer at least two examples in each of these areas.

Stress does not affect everybody in the same way. Here you are required to show your understanding of how the effects of stress might be modified by **personality differences** (e.g. the Type A and non-Type A difference demonstrated by Friedman and Rosenman), **cultural differences** and **gender differences**.

Stress and life events

Life events are transitional events (such as divorce or bereavement) that require a significant adjustment in various aspects of a person's life. Research in this area has attempted to explore the relationship between these events and the development of stress-related disorders (such as depression).

Holmes and Rahe (1967) — the social readjustment rating scale (SRRS)

Holmes and Rahe developed this scale to explore whether the development of stress-related disorders might be explained in terms of the number of stressful life events experienced by people prior to development of the disorder.

They asked men and women to rate 43 life events in terms of the psychological readjustment they would require. Death of a spouse was given the highest rating of

100 and marriage was given a rating of 50. After constructing the scale, they then asked participants to indicate which of the events they had experienced over the previous 2 years. The total score was used as an indication of the stress in that person's life.

Holmes and Rahe discovered that people who had a score of 150 or more were 30% more likely to be suffering from a stress-related health problem than those with scores below 150. For those with scores in excess of 300, this increased the odds by 50%.

Use of the SRRS typically shows small but significant correlations between life events and health problems, suggesting a link between stress and health, albeit not a strong one.

Evaluation
- This relationship is only correlational and tells us nothing about causality, and the results from the SRRS cannot distinguish between events that might be positive (such as marriage) and those that might be negative (such as divorce).

Workplace stressors

Work overload (Johansson et al., 1978)

Johansson et al.'s study of employees in a Swedish timber mill aimed to explore whether work that was machine-paced generated significant stress reactions in those who were most affected by the consequent work overload.

They studied the 'finishers' in the timber mill — men who were responsible for the final stages of the timber preparation process and as such were responsible for the overall productivity of the workforce. The researchers measured levels of stress hormones during work days and rest days, and took other measurements such as sickness and absenteeism.

These workers had raised levels of stress hormones on work days and a higher incidence of stress-related health problems than other workers in the process. They also showed higher levels of absenteeism than the other workers at the sawmill.

The researchers concluded that the work environment of these workers was stressful because they were responsible for the wages of the whole factory, their work was boring and repetitive, and, as their work was machine-paced, they lacked any control over their work environment.

Evaluation
+ The findings of this study are valuable in that they suggest work practices (e.g. job rotation and greater control) that would reduce stress in the workplace.

Role-related responsibility (Cobb and Rose, 1973)

Cobb and Rose investigated role-related stress in male air-traffic controllers. They wanted to find out whether jobs that entailed significant role responsibilities would be more stressful than those that did not.

The researchers compared the incidence of various illnesses among a group of air-traffic controllers and a control group of other airmen. The data were provided as a result of compulsory medical examinations that were necessary when the men were renewing their licences.

They found, after adjusting for age, that the air-traffic controllers were four times as likely to be suffering from hypertension (raised blood pressure) than the airmen in the control group. They also showed a significantly higher incidence of diabetes and peptic ulcers than those in the control group.

The researchers found that the air-traffic controllers needed to exercise almost continuous attention, often having to work with very low-quality information, rapidly and without error. The heavy responsibility of their role appeared to have a heavy cost in terms of their lower levels of health.

Evaluation

– This study has only demonstrated the relationship between work role responsibility and stress in males. Research suggests that females may show different reactions to stress.

Individual differences in modifying the effects of stressors

Personality — Type A behaviour

Friedman and Rosenman (1974) studied the behaviour of people who were suffering from coronary heart disease (CHD) and found that they displayed a particular type of behaviour pattern that was characterised by being under constant time pressure, intensely competitive and easily frustrated by the efforts of others. They called this the **Type A behaviour pattern**, and claimed that there was a link between this and the incidence of CHD.

Although studies have found significant correlations between the two, these tend to be small. It has also been suggested that people high in repressed hostility *and* Type A are more vulnerable to CHD than those who show Type A alone. One reason why Type A people do not necessarily develop CHD is the high degree of *control* they exercise over their lives.

Gender

There is evidence that the sexes react differently to stressful situations. Stoney et al. (1990) found that women showed much smaller increases in blood pressure compared with men during stressful situations. This might indicate that the stress pathways of women are less reactive than those of men, or alternatively, it may show that men and women differ in their attitude to stressful situations, with men being more competitive and more aroused by competitive situations.

Gender differences in reactions to stress could be the result of evolutionary differences between the sexes (Taylor, 2000), such as the tendency for females to seek social contact during times of stress. This might be linked to the action of the hormone oxytocin (higher levels in women) which is released at times of stress, and which makes us calmer and more social. Eagley (2000) disagrees, saying that differences in the way that males and females deal with stress have nothing to do with biological factors but are simply a part of the gender–role socialisation that males and females experience as they grow up.

Culture

Although stress is found in all cultures, the source of stress, and the way in which people deal with it, may be different, depending on the culture being studied.

Social support appears to be one of the most important factors that protects against the negative effects of stress. Research by Kim and McKenry (1998) found strong cultural differences in the degree to which members of different cultures relied on family or other close relationships for social support.

Because of the difficulties of making comparisons across cultures, it is hard to disentangle the effects of stress and stress management from other factors that might prolong or shorten life. Research by Weg (1983), among the Abkarsian people of Georgia, found that their longevity could be explained by a combination of factors, including genetic inheritance, high levels of social support, physically active lifestyles, no alcohol or smoking and low reported stress levels.

Critical issue: stress management

Specification content

Methods of managing the negative effects of stress, including physiological (e.g. drugs, biofeedback) and psychological approaches (e.g. the work of Meichenbaum on stress-inoculation and Kobasa on increasing hardiness). The role of 'control' in the perception of stress. The strengths and weaknesses of methods of stress management.

The use of the word '*methods*' in the plural tells you that you should be prepared for questions that might ask for more than one *psychological* method and more than one *physiological* method of stress management. You should, however, also be prepared to write about just one method in sufficient depth for a 6-mark (i.e. 6 minutes) question. The examples given are just that — examples. There are other examples of each approach that would be relevant. Make sure you are clear about the *difference* between a physical and a psychological approach to stress management.

The role of **control** in the perception of stress requires you to know how control (e.g. through the nature of the stressor itself or through personality differences) alters the experience and effects of stress.

You are also required to know about the *strengths* and *weaknesses* of each of your chosen methods of stress management as well as being able to summarise these in an overview of the strengths and weaknesses of physical and psychological methods in general.

Physical approaches

Drugs

Commonly used drugs that are used to combat stress are:

- benzodiazepine (BZ) anti-anxiety drugs such as Librium and Valium, which work by reducing the activity of the neurotransmitter **serotonin**
- beta-blockers, which work by reducing activity in the pathways of the sympathetic nervous system, and therefore are effective against raised heart rate and blood pressure

Evaluation

- Long-term use of BZs can actually erode a person's ability to deal with stress, leading to greater dependence on the drugs. Therefore, although BZs can offer short-term relief from the negative effects of stress, over the longer term they might be less useful.
- Drugs treat the symptoms of stress, not the causes. Most stressors are psychological; therefore, physical measures do not address the real cause of the problem.

Biofeedback

This is a technique for controlling physiological responses by receiving information about the body's stress response as it occurs. Monitoring devices track physiological responses such as heart rate and blood pressure. These provide the person with feedback in the form of a light or tone whenever they change the response in the desired direction. The aim of this technique is to find a strategy to reduce a particular stress-related response which can then be transferred to the outside world and used regularly to relieve stress.

Evaluation

+ It is claimed that biofeedback techniques can have significant positive effects in the reduction of generalised anxiety disorders.
- Use of this technique and the related efforts to reduce heart rate in sufferers of anxiety disorders have had only limited success.
- Biofeedback might be no more effective than muscle relaxation in the absence of biofeedback. This is a critical issue, as biofeedback can be expensive as a technique.

Psychological approaches

Psychological approaches to stress can be either **general**, such as using relaxation techniques or meditation to reduce the body's state of arousal, or **specific**, using cognitive and behavioural training.

Relaxation techniques

Progressive muscle relaxation is an active approach to reducing bodily arousal. A client is trained to tense and relax muscles progressively, working up the body from the legs to the facial muscles. Eventually they can use the technique as a way of reducing bodily arousal. During the relaxation state, stress response mechanisms are inactive and the parasympathetic nervous system is dominant.

Evaluation

+ It is fairly easy to practise relaxation, even in the most unusual circumstances. These techniques may also involve cognitive strategies that help reduce arousal in unpleasantly arousing circumstances.
− Although relaxation techniques can be useful by reducing the levels of stress response, their action is non-specific. Effective long-term stress reduction requires intervention focused on the source of the stress.

Meditation

This technique is similar to relaxation in that the aim of the technique is to reduce bodily arousal and achieve a state of inner calm. During meditation, a person is trained to repeat their mantra (a sound or single word) while breathing deeply and regularly. By doing this, the person is able to rid their mind of the arousing thoughts that activate the body's stress response system.

Evaluation

+ Meditation has the advantage of 'portability' and could give individuals more confidence to deal with stressful situations.
− As with relaxation techniques, the action of meditation techniques is non-specific, rather than focused on effective intervention at source.

Meichenbaum's stress-inoculation training

This technique has three phases:

- **conceptualisation** — the cognitive element, where the client is encouraged to relive stressful situations, analysing what was stressful about them and how they attempted to deal with them
- **skills training and practice** — the client is taught a variety of techniques (e.g. relaxation, social skills, time management) in the therapeutic setting
- **real-life application** — the client can put what they have learned into practice in the real world; reinforcement of techniques learned in therapy makes the practices self-sustaining

Evaluation

+ Meichenbaum's model focuses on both the nature of the stress problem (enabling clients to appraise their life more realistically) and ways of coping with stress (giving clients more understanding of the strengths and limitations of specific techniques).
+ The combination of cognitive strategies and behavioural techniques makes stress-inoculation a potentially effective way of managing stress.
− Despite this potential, few controlled studies have confirmed its predictions.

Hardiness (Kobasa and Maddi, 1977)

The concept of 'hardiness' is taken to mean resistance to illness, or ability to deal with stress. Kobasa and Maddi were able to identify the characteristics of those who handled stress well from those who did not. Those who reported the fewest illnesses showed three kinds of hardiness:

- openness to change, i.e. life changes are seen as challenges to be overcome rather than threats or stressors (Kobasa and Maddi believed this to be the most important factor)
- a feeling of involvement or commitment to their job, and a sense of purpose in their activities
- a sense of control over their lives, rather than seeing their lives controlled by outside influences

Kobasa and Maddi proposed three ways in which hardiness could be improved:
- **focusing** — the client is trained to recognise stressful situations and therefore to identify the sources of stress
- **reliving stressful encounters** — the client analyses past coping and realises their techniques are more effective than they thought
- **self-improvement** — a central aspect of hardiness is that we can cope with life's challenges — clients are encouraged to take on challenges that they can cope with, thus reinforcing feelings of control

Evaluation

+ The relative importance of the three aspects of hardiness (control, commitment and challenge) is uncertain, although it is likely that control is the most significant of these.
− Kobasa and Maddi's studies have tended to involve middle-class businessmen — results cannot reliably be generalised to other social and cultural groups.

Effectiveness — the importance of other factors

- **Previous experience** — once we have experienced a particular stressful situation, we are usually able to cope better with it if it recurs. The experience provides us with knowledge about the situation and makes it more predictable.
- **Individual differences** — some people try to protect themselves from the full impact of the stress by denying, playing down or emotionally detaching themselves from the situation. Providing information to these people can actually increase their stress levels, rather than decrease them.
- **Social support** — the impact of stressful events is affected by our social systems. Response to stress can be eased by support from either the family or the community. For example, studies have shown that women who have close, confiding relationships are less likely to develop stress-related psychiatric disorders.
- **Control** — the degree to which we believe we can control a situation has an important impact on the degree to which that situation is likely to cause us stress. The most harmful and distressing situations are those in which we feel entirely helpless, believing that nothing we can do will significantly alter the outcome. The role of control in the experience of stress is expanded below.

The role of control

Karasek (1979) carried out an analysis of US and Swedish studies of stress at work, and found that employees in jobs perceived to have both low decision latitude (i.e. low levels of personal control) and high job demands were particularly likely to report poor health and low satisfaction. The lowest probabilities of illness and death were found among work groups with moderate workloads combined with high control over work conditions.

Criticisms have been levelled against Karasek's model (the 'demand–control model'). For example, it has been claimed that the model is too simple and ignores the moderating effect of social support (e.g. from co-workers and supervisors) on these variables. Social support seems to play an essential role in the management of stress at work. It serves as a buffer against possible adverse health effects of excessive psychological demands.

Individual differences can exist in relation to the person's perception of job demands and pressures. Hartley (1987) found a positive correlation between perceptions of the severity of problems facing unemployed men and a measure of locus of control. The more they believed that important life events were not under their personal control, the more severe they perceived their problems to be. However, people vary in the amount of control that they can exercise over any situation, not only as a function of that situation but also as a function of their beliefs about control.

The issue of control is important in understanding the nature of Type A behaviour. The Type A individual feels that they are always fighting to maintain control over events, which are often seen to be just beyond their grasp. They can expend more time and effort trying to 'get events under control', and never really feel as if they have succeeded. The issue of control, and of being in control, is an important one and distinguishes between the vulnerability of Type As and the resistance of hardy types (Kobasa, 1979). Type A behaviour predicts cardiovascular ill health, while hardiness predicts general good health.

Coping is an important part of the overall stress process, and gaining control can be seen as part of a wider problem-solving strategy. Lazarus (1966) argued that a person can employ both task- and emotion-focused coping strategies when faced with a stressful situation. The former involves some form of action directly targeted at dealing with the source of stress (adaptation to the environment through problem-solving activities), while the latter attempts to lessen the emotional experience associated with that stress (adaptation to the environment through altering one's emotional appraisal of an event).

Stress: defining the terms

cardiovascular disorders: disorders relating to the heart and blood vessels. This can be evident in physical damage to the blood supply system, which might in turn lead to the gradual blocking of a blood vessel (atherosclerosis).

control: the ability to anticipate things that might happen in one's environment, as well as perceiving oneself as actively being able to control those events when they do happen. The most stressful situations appear to be those where we feel entirely helpless, believing that nothing we do will change the outcome of events.

general adaptation syndrome: this proposes that there are three stages in our response to long-term stress: the alarm stage, where the sympathetic branch of the autonomic nervous system is activated; the resistance stage, where the body attempts to cope by maintaining the same level of arousal; and the exhaustion stage, where the body's resources and defence against the stressor become exhausted.

immune system: a system of cells within the body that is concerned with fighting against intruders such as viruses and bacteria. White blood cells (leucocytes) identify and kill foreign bodies (called antigens).

life changes: events (such as divorce or bereavement) that necessitate a significant adjustment in various aspects of a person's life. As such, they can be seen as significant sources of stress.

physical approaches to stress management: the use of techniques (such as drugs and biofeedback) designed to change the activity of the body's stress response system.

psychological approaches to stress management: the use of techniques (such as relaxation, hypnosis, or specific cognitive–behavioural techniques such as stress-inoculation) that are designed to help people cope better with stressful situations or to alter their perception of the demands of a stressful situation.

stress: this can be defined as a characteristic of the environment (e.g. workplace stress), as the response of the body to a stressful situation, or as the lack of fit between a person and their environment (i.e. where the perceived demands of a situation are greater than the perceived ability to cope).

stress management: the different ways in which people try to cope with the negative effects of stress. We might attempt to change the way our body responds to stress (the physical approach) or change our relationship with the stressful situation (the psychological approach).

stressor: events that cause a stress reaction in the body. These include environmental stressors such as workplace stressors or examinations, and life events such as divorce or bereavement.

workplace stressor: an aspect of our working environment (such as work overload, impending deadlines or role ambiguity) that we experience as stressful and which causes a stress reaction in our body.

Individual differences: abnormality

Defining psychological abnormality

Specification content

Attempts to define abnormality in terms of statistical infrequency, deviation from social norms, a 'failure to function adequately' and deviation from ideal mental health. Limitations associated with these attempts to define psychological abnormality (including cultural relativism).

This subsection requires you both to *define* and to *criticise* (i.e. offer *limitations* for) the four definitions listed above. Note that this includes **cultural relativism** (the view that one must take into account the cultural context of a behaviour before judging its abnormality).

Statistical infrequency

Most human characteristics (including personality traits and behaviour) fall within a normal distribution, with most people clustering around the middle of the distribution (i.e. the norm), and fewer and fewer towards the edges. Any characteristic that is statistically rare according to this distribution is considered abnormal.

> **Evaluation**
> - Some behaviours are statistically infrequent (such as exceptional musical talent), yet are not classified as 'abnormal'. Judging which behaviours are infrequent and abnormal (as opposed to infrequent and normal) must involve some other criterion.
> - Identifying mental disorders as examples of abnormality under this definition might be inappropriate. Depression and anxiety disorders may be widespread in some cultures, yet relatively absent in others. This might reflect cultural differences in seeking help for disorders rather than differences in their occurrence.

Deviation from social norms

What is considered abnormal is any behaviour that deviates from a social (rather than a statistical) norm. These are implicit 'rules' about how we ought to behave (e.g. talking to ourselves in public), and violation of these rules is considered 'deviant' or 'abnormal'. These rules reflect the moral standards of a particular culture; therefore, under this definition, what is considered abnormal will differ from culture to culture.

> **Evaluation**
> - Social norms change over time rather than being fixed and unchangeable. For example, homosexuality was classified as a mental disorder in the DSM classification until 1973.
> - Attempts to diagnose abnormality in the UK might show evidence of 'cultural

blindness'. The characteristics of the White population are treated as normative and the behaviour of other racial or ethnic groups is interpreted as being indicative of some underlying abnormality.

Failure to function adequately

People who are mentally healthy are typically seen as functioning within certain acceptable limits (e.g. being able to look after oneself, or being able to carry on normal social discourse). If a person's behaviour interferes with their ability to operate within those limits, then it could be classified as abnormal. Behaviour that is bizarre (such as having hallucinations), inefficient (such as being unable to leave the house because of obsessions) or which might be considered unpredictable or incomprehensible to others, might be defined as abnormal.

Evaluation

- Some apparently dysfunctional behaviour might be adaptive and functional for the individual. For example, panic attacks can ensure that the person receives previously unobtainable attention from others (the so-called 'neurotic paradox').
- Some disorders are more prevalent in women than in men. Women appear to be more vulnerable to depression, yet this could be more a product of socio-cultural (rather than individual) factors. By labelling this a 'mental disorder', clinicians are stigmatising the person rather than the socio-cultural context that produced the depression.

Deviation from ideal mental health

First proposed by Jahoda (1958), this definition focuses on the major criteria of *positive* mental health. If a person deviated from one or more of these criteria, they would be vulnerable to a mental disorder. The six criteria are: positive attitude to the self (i.e. having self-respect and self-acceptance); self-actualisation of one's potential; resistance to stress (i.e. having developed good coping strategies for stress); personal autonomy (i.e. being able to make decisions on the basis of what is right for ourselves rather than others); accurate perception of reality (i.e. seeing the world in realistic terms); and adapting to the environment (i.e. being flexible and able to adjust to change).

Evaluation

- Most people, according to this definition, would fall short of ideal mental health, yet would not be considered to possess an 'abnormality'. Defining abnormality in these terms might create anxiety in those who are otherwise mentally healthy.
- Although it is possible to measure ideal physical health with reasonable objectivity, measuring ideal mental health with the same degree of objectivity is more difficult because the criteria are more vague.

Cultural relativism

Each of the definitions detailed above is subject to the influence of culture. Berry et al. (1992) suggest that abnormal conditions may be **absolute** (occurring in the same way and with the same frequency in all cultures), **universal** (occurring in all cultures but not with the same frequency) or **relative** (unique to particular cultures and only meaningful within those cultures). Conditions that appear only in certain cultures are referred to as

culture-bound syndromes. Although these are recognised as illnesses within those cultures, they might not fit any recognised Western category of mental disorder.

Within cultures, sub-groups (or **subcultures**) can likewise differ in their experience of mental disorders. Wadeley et al. (2000) summarise these subcultures as:

- **gender** — women are more often diagnosed as suffering from depression and anxiety disorders than are men, and more attention is paid to the role of hormones in women's mental health (e.g. PMS) than in men's mental health. However, statistical data might reflect more the differences between male and female socialisation (including attitudes towards seeking help) than real differences between the sexes.
- **race** — some groups (such as African-Caribbeans) are more likely to receive diagnoses of major mental disorders (such as schizophrenia). Cochrane and Sashidharan (1995) suggest that diagnosis in the UK is 'culturally blind', with the behaviours of the White population being treated as normative. Any deviation from this is seen as indicative of an underlying pathology.
- **social class** — members of socially disadvantaged groups are more likely to be diagnosed with a major mental disorder. This could be a product of their more stressful life experiences, or a consequence of **social drift**, where the early onset of a mental disorder causes a downward spiral in the person's life chances. Social class then becomes a consequence of, rather than a contributory factor in, the diagnosis of a mental disorder.

Biological and psychological models of abnormality

Specification content

Assumptions made by biological (medical) and psychological (including psychodynamic, behavioural and cognitive) models of abnormality in terms of their views on the causes and treatment of abnormality.

Assumptions are beliefs that are held without proof. You should know two or three assumptions for each model of abnormality. There are *four* models specified above (**biological, psychodynamic, behavioural** and **cognitive**). Note that there are two different kinds of assumptions — those relating to the *causes* of abnormality, and those relating to its *treatment*. The latter is not an invitation to describe specific treatments, but to consider, in broad terms, how such views of the causes of abnormality might be translated into its treatment.

The biological (medical) model

Assumptions of the causes of abnormality

The basic assumption of the biological model is that mental disorders are caused by abnormal physiological processes. By using family and twin studies, it is possible to investigate the possible influence of genetic factors in a given disorder. In most disorders that have a genetic influence (such as schizophrenia), people inherit the **genotype**, whereas the symptoms of the disorder are the **phenotype**. Whether or not a person who is genetically predisposed to a specific disorder develops the symptoms of the disorder is determined by a number of other factors. Biochemical explanations propose that many disorders might be explained in terms of dysfunctions in **neurotransmitter** action. For example, depression might be caused by a lowered level of activity in the neurotransmitters **serotonin** or **noradrenaline**, whereas an excess of **dopamine** activity is thought to be responsible for many of the symptoms of schizophrenia.

Implications for treatment

As mental disorders are seen essentially as physical illnesses, the major implication of this approach is that alterations in bodily functioning (through drugs, ECT or psychosurgery) will be effective in the treatment and prevention of these disorders. If a disorder (such as depression) is a product of neurotransmitter dysfunction, then it should be possible to stabilise the condition by the use of drug treatments that restore normal neurotransmitter activity. Likewise, sedatives, such as Valium, can be used to reduce tension in anxiety disorders.

The use of psychosurgery reflects the belief that some disorders have their roots in the abnormal functioning of a specific area of the brain. Through surgical intervention, it is believed, it becomes possible to change a psychological condition.

> **Evaluation**
>
> + Because of the sophisticated research techniques that are possible with this approach, research into the biological aspects of abnormality progresses rapidly, with new information concerning the causes of a mental disorder such as schizophrenia, together with insights into its treatment, being gained in a relatively short time. These insights can likewise be tested scientifically, so that a greater degree of certainty concerning the claims of this model is possible compared with other models of abnormality.
> − The evidence for biological explanations of abnormality is often incomplete or inconclusive. Many studies must be carried out on animals, yet researchers cannot be certain that these animals are experiencing the disorder under investigation, merely that they are reacting in an abnormal way. Similarly, evidence for the genetic basis of certain abnormalities is open to alternative interpretations that are more 'experiential' than biological.

The psychodynamic model

Assumptions of the causes of abnormality

Psychodynamic models see abnormal behaviour as being caused by underlying psychological forces of which the person is probably unaware, often originating from childhood experiences. In Freudian theory, the personality is made up of three interacting systems:

- the **id**, present at birth, pleasure-oriented and constantly striving for expression
- the **superego**, the moral part of the personality containing the ego-ideal and conscience
- the **ego**, operating on the reality principle, which must arbitrate between the conflicting demands of the id and the superego

A well-adjusted person develops a strong ego, allowing both the id and superego expression at appropriate times. If the conflict between id and superego is not managed effectively, the person experiences a psychological disturbance (for example, an unrestrained id can produce psychopathic behaviour in adulthood).

Although psychological conflicts can occur at any time of life, they are most evident in early childhood when the ego is insufficiently developed to mediate in this battle between id and superego. It is not sufficiently developed to cope with the emotional disturbances caused by (for example) parental absence or sibling rivalry. Such experiences can be repressed into the unconscious mind where they eventually re-emerge in later psychological problems. Freud believed that nobody was completely free from such conflicts; therefore, we are all 'abnormal' to some extent.

Implications for treatment

Psychodynamic therapies such as Freudian psychoanalysis attempt to uncover unconscious processes which will, in turn, enable the therapist to gain insight into the underlying conflicts or anxieties that are causing the current psychological problem. During psychoanalytic therapy, the aim is to create appropriate conditions so that the client is able to bring these conflicts into the conscious mind where they might be addressed and dealt with.

If a person can understand the reasons for their current abnormal behaviour, then, according to the assumptions of this approach to treatment, they should be better able to deal with both the original problem and the current problems for which they sought treatment.

Evaluation

- Some critics of psychoanalysis claim that those who undertake psychoanalysis fare little better in terms of improvement than those who do not undertake any form of therapy over the same period of time.
- Psychoanalysis appears to benefit only certain types of patient (particularly those who are highly motivated and have a positive attitude to therapy) and is less effective in patients with severe psychopathological problems.

The behavioural model

Assumptions of the causes of abnormality

The behavioural model sees abnormality as the development of maladaptive behaviour patterns that are established through the principles of learning, namely classical and operant conditioning, and modelling. Classical conditioning explanations of abnormal behaviour stress the **associations** that are learned between two stimuli (the original fear evoking stimulus and a neutral stimulus with which it is paired). Through repeated associations the neutral stimulus acquires the same ability to produce a fear response as the original stimulus.

Operant conditioning explanations stress the role of **reinforcement** in abnormal behaviour, with many apparently maladaptive behaviours developing because they produce a desired response from others. Through modelling, a child might develop maladaptive behaviours as a result of its exposure to the same behaviours in significant others (such as parents).

Implications for treatment

Because the behavioural model focuses on abnormal **behaviour**, therapies based on this model treat people according to their **symptoms** rather than trying to establish the underlying causes of a behaviour. Behaviourists believe that maladaptive behaviours are acquired using the same learning processes that produce normal behaviours (i.e. classical and operant conditioning, and modelling); therefore these same techniques can be used to change these problematic behaviours.

The goal of behavioural treatment is to identify the specific maladaptive behaviours and manipulate them so that they are replaced by more constructive behaviours. The removal of the symptoms is then seen as the criterion of improvement and of the effectiveness of the behavioural treatment.

Evaluation

+ One of the attractions of the behavioural model and its treatments is that it can be tested scientifically. Experimental work has demonstrated in the laboratory that, using behaviourist learning principles, it is possible to produce the symptoms of abnormal functioning in individuals. Similarly, in clinical psychology, the effectiveness of behavioural treatments can be demonstrated using the criteria for improvement outlined above.

– Some critics of the behavioural model argue that, because of its focus on overt behaviours, it is too simplistic, and fails to acknowledge the complexity of human behaviour. In particular, people's ability to think critically about their behaviour is largely ignored in this view of abnormality.

The cognitive model

Assumptions of the causes of abnormality

The cognitive model stresses the role of irrational thought processes as a basis for abnormal functioning. These include **maladaptive assumptions** about ourselves (such as the belief that there is a 'perfect' solution to all life's problems), **specific upsetting thoughts** (fleeting thoughts and images that occur 'automatically' in our thought processes) and **illogical thinking processes** (such as 'selective perception', where we see only the negative features of an event, and 'magnification', where we exaggerate the importance of undesirable experiences). Cognitive theorists believe that most abnormal behaviour is caused by inappropriate or counterproductive thinking rather than being caused by an illness.

Implications for treatment

According to the cognitive model, abnormal functioning is a consequence of inappropriate and counterproductive thought processes. The goal of cognitive therapy, therefore, is to help people recognise these faulty thought processes and to change them to more appropriate and productive ways of thinking about themselves and their world. Because the cognitive approach to treatment helps people to develop more realistic views of their world, it offers a 'model for living' that promotes psychological well-being and avoids the stigma of mental illness (Prentice, 2000).

Evaluation

+ The cognitive view of abnormality is also testable scientifically. Research has established that people with psychological disorders (most notably depression and anxiety disorders) *do* display the irrational thought processes predicted by this model. Similarly, when experimental manipulations of individuals' thought processes cause them to think in this way, they become more anxious and depressed (Rimm and Litvak, 1969).

− Although abnormal thought processes can be shown to be a feature of abnormal functioning, their precise role is not clear. It is possible that such maladaptive ways of thinking are a *consequence* of a disorder such as depression, rather than being the *cause* of it.

Critical issue: eating disorders

Specification content

The clinical characteristics of anorexia nervosa and bulimia nervosa. Explanations of these disorders in terms of biological and psychological models of abnormality, including research studies on which these explanations are based.

The requirement here is to cover the *characteristics* of anorexia nervosa and bulimia nervosa (e.g. the symptoms and aetiology), *explanations* (biological and psychological) and *research studies* relating to these explanations. It is wise to cover more than one *biological* explanation (e.g. the influence of genes and biochemical explanations) and more than one *psychological* explanation (e.g. psychodynamic and behavioural). Questions might also ask for *differences* between anorexia nervosa and bulimia nervosa, and you might be asked to *evaluate* the explanations you have given.

Clinical characteristics of anorexia nervosa (DSM-IV)

- Refusal to maintain body weight at or above minimal normal weight for age and height, or failure to make expected weight gain during periods of growth, leading to body weight of less than 85% of that expected.
- Intense fear of becoming fat, despite being underweight.
- Disturbance in the way that one's body weight or shape is experienced; undue influence of body weight or shape on self-evaluation; denial of seriousness of current low body weight.

- In post-menarchal girls (those who have begun to menstruate), the absence of three consecutive menstrual cycles.

Clinical characteristics of bulimia nervosa (DSM-IV)

- Recurrent episodes of binge eating.
- Recurrent and inappropriate compensatory behaviours to prevent weight gain, including vomiting, the use of laxatives or excessive exercise.
- Binge eating and compensatory behaviours occurring, on average, at least twice a week for a period of 3 months or more.
- Self-evaluation is unduly influenced by body shape and weight.
- The disturbance is not part of a larger pattern of anorexia nervosa.

The differences between anorexia nervosa and bulimia nervosa, according to Comer (1995), are outlined in the following table.

Anorexia nervosa	Bulimia nervosa
Refusal to maintain healthy body weight	Under- or overweight or in between
Hunger and disorder denied	Awareness of hunger and disorder
Less antisocial behaviour	More antisocial behaviour
Amenorrhoea (cessation of menstruation)	Irregular menstruation common
Family conflict denied	Intense family conflict perceived

Biological explanations of eating disorders

The influence of genes

Results from *family studies* have shown that there is an increased risk of eating disorders among first-degree relatives (parents, children and siblings) of individuals with an eating disorder than among the general population.

Holland et al. (1984) found a 55% concordance rate (the percentage of twins who, if their twin has an eating disorder, also have it) for MZ (genetically identical) twins, compared with only 7% for DZ (as alike as siblings, but not identical) twins.

> **Evaluation**
> + Although there are significantly higher concordance rates for MZ twins than for DZ twins, this still leaves a large percentage of twins where the 'other' twin of an affected individual does not develop an eating disorder (Prentice, 2000).
> − Hsu (1990) suggests that the genetic element of eating disorders might relate more to personality traits, such as emotional instability, which make such individuals more susceptible to life events.

The role of the hypothalamus

The influence of the hypothalamus in hunger and satiation in animals is well documented. There are two major areas of the hypothalamus that control eating:

- the lateral hypothalamus (LH) produces hunger when it is activated
- the ventromedial hypothalamus (VMH) depresses hunger when it is activated

It is believed that the LH and VMH work together to set up a 'weight thermostat' which maintains a set point for weight (the normal weight for that person, determined by genetic inheritance, early eating practices, etc.). If the 'thermostat' rises above this point, the VMH is activated; if weight falls below the weight set point, the LH is activated. A malfunction in the hypothalamus might explain eating disorders.

Evaluation

- Although the role of the hypothalamus in the eating behaviour of animals is well documented, there is little conclusive evidence that eating orders might be influenced in the same way in humans.
- It is not clear why some people manage to gain control over the compensatory mechanisms necessary to maintain the correct weight level, while others become caught in a cycle of bingeing and purging. It seems likely that the psychological differences between anorexia and bulimia sufferers are important in this respect.

Illustrative research study into the biological basis of eating disorders (Strober et al., 2000)

Strober et al. (2000) compared the incidence of anorexia nervosa and bulimia nervosa in genetic relatives of probands diagnosed with anorexia or bulimia, with relatives of matched comparison subjects without an eating disorder, in order to investigate whether these disorders might be inherited. (A **proband** is the individual who is the starting point for a genetic study of a family.) Note that this study can be used for anorexia *and* bulimia.

The rates of each eating disorder were obtained for 1831 first-degree relatives of 504 probands on the basis of clinical interviews and family history. Estimates of diagnosis based on all available information were given without knowledge of proband status or the identity of the person being assessed.

Whereas anorexia nervosa was rare in families of the comparison subjects (those who did not have an eating disorder), the incidence of anorexia nervosa was concentrated in female relatives of both anorexic and bulimic probands. Bulimia nervosa was more common than anorexia nervosa in female relatives of comparison subjects, but it, too, was concentrated mainly in the families of those who suffered from either anorexia or bulimia nervosa.

This led researchers to conclude that both anorexia nervosa and bulimia nervosa run in families. Their cross-transmission in families suggests a common, or shared, familial vulnerability to these disorders.

Evaluation

- Research suggests that it is not eating disorders that are inherited, but rather an obsessional personality that makes people more vulnerable to such disorders.

Psychological explanations of eating disorders

Behaviourist explanations

Using the principles of classical and operant conditioning, dieting and the quest for thinness might be seen as a habit, with the individual associating thinness with the admiration of others or with feelings of positive well-being. As other people frequently provide reinforcement for the new 'thin' person, the refusal to eat becomes an effective way of gaining such 'rewards'.

The media can also cause people to develop distorted views of what is a 'normal' body image. Through dieting and exercise a person may strive to achieve the 'idealised' body that they see modelled in the media. As body weight drops below a critical point, eating disorders such as anorexia nervosa may be triggered.

Evaluation

+ Behaviourist explanations may help to explain gender differences in eating disorders. The emphasis on appearance and the pressure to be thin (a characteristic of Western societies) is aimed more at women than men. This has resulted in women being more concerned with being thin, more inclined to diet, and therefore more vulnerable to eating disorders.
+ Research has shown that if a person travels from a culture where thin images are rare to a culture where they are more widespread, that person will begin to become more aware of his/her image and start comparing him/herself to that 'ideal' image. This supports the behaviourist claim that people are influenced by the images they are exposed to in the media.

Psychodynamic explanations

Psychodynamic explanations tend to stress the role of disturbed parent–child relationships in the development of eating disorders. For example, Bruch (1974) claimed that ineffective parents, instead of responding appropriately to the needs of their children (e.g. by giving them food when they cry in hunger), impose their own wishes on the child and attend to their needs in arbitrary ways. They might feed them when they are anxious, comfort them when they are hungry and so on. Their children are thus unable to differentiate between their own internal needs and fail to develop self-reliance. To overcome this sense of helplessness, the adolescent tries to control their body size and shape in a desperate attempt to exert some personal control over their lives. Some are 'successful' and become anorexic, while others develop the binge and purge cycle of bulimia.

Evaluation

– As with many psychodynamic explanations, Bruch's views on the causes of eating disorders lack objectivity. The conflicts commonly found between the anorexic and their family might be the *consequence* of an eating disorder rather than its *cause*.
– Conflicts between parents and their children, and the 'ineffective' parenting described by Bruch, have been evident throughout history, yet eating disorders such as anorexia nervosa and bulimia nervosa are fairly recent occurrences.

Illustrative research study into the psychological basis of anorexia nervosa (Davis et al., 1997)

Numerous studies have found that subjective physical attractiveness is inversely related to weight and diet concerns. This research investigated the relationship between objective physical beauty and the incidence of anorexia nervosa.

Davis et al. rated 203 young women on facial attractiveness and also obtained self-report measures of other characteristics, such as perfectionism, neuroticism and weight preoccupation.

Attractiveness was positively related to weight preoccupation after controlling for body size and neurotic perfectionism. Women who scored higher on objective measures of facial attractiveness also tended to show a greater preoccupation with their weight.

These findings provide the first evidence of physical beauty as a risk for anorexia nervosa, and also demonstrate that a relationship between general perfectionism and disordered eating only occurs when combined with a tendency to be anxious and hypercritical.

Evaluation

+ The value of this study lies in the fact that it highlights the complex origins of anorexia rather than seeing it as an automatic consequence of one aspect of personality.

Illustrative research study on the psychological basis of bulimia nervosa (Wonderlich and Wilsnack, 1996)

Aims

This study investigated whether childhood sexual abuse was a significant risk factor in the development of bulimic behaviour in women; specifically whether sexually abused women would display all three of the major criteria for bulimia nervosa, i.e. binge-eating, purging and excessive weight concern.

Procedure

Interviews were conducted among a representative national sample of 1099 US women as part of a national survey on drinking behaviour. Female interviewers asked questions regarding the women's sexual experiences during childhood as well as any experience of bulimic behaviour. Researchers controlled for the respondents' age, ethnic group, and parents' educational level.

Results

Twenty-four per cent of the women interviewed were classified as having been sexually abused in childhood. Binge-eating, by itself or in combination with counter-active behaviours such as purging, was two or more times more prevalent among the women who had experienced childhood sexual abuse than among the women who had not. In contrast, heightened concerns about weight and body shape were not related as strongly to childhood sexual abuse.

Conclusions

This study found evidence that childhood sexual abuse is a risk factor for bulimic behaviour in adulthood. Between one-sixth and one-third of the cases of significant bulimic disturbance found in the study could be attributed to childhood sexual abuse.

Evaluation

- Although this study found a significant relationship between one aspect of bulimia (binge-eating) and early childhood abuse, the prediction that victims of childhood sexual abuse would be more concerned about body shape and weight than non-victims was not supported. The high prevalence of weight concerns among the women interviewed suggests that weight preoccupation may be so common that it has many causes unrelated to childhood sexual abuse.
- The observed relationship between childhood sexual abuse and adult bulimia nervosa may be inflated if bulimic patients, in an 'effort after meaning', search their lives for an explanation for their bulimia. Consequently, they remember or report childhood sexual abuse more often than do control subjects, who lack such explanatory motivation.

Abnormality: defining the terms

abnormality: a psychological condition or behaviour that departs from the norm or that is harmful and distressing to the individual or those around them. Abnormal behaviours are usually those that violate society's ideas of what is an appropriate level of functioning.

anorexia nervosa: a type of eating disorder in which the person, despite being seriously underweight, fears that they might become obese and therefore engages in self-starvation to prevent this happening.

bulimia nervosa: a type of eating disorder in which a person habitually engages in episodes of uncontrollable eating (known as bingeing) followed by self-induced vomiting or other compensatory behaviours. Bulimics have an abnormal concern with body size and a morbid fear of being or becoming fat.

cultural relativism: the view that behaviour cannot be judged properly unless it is viewed in the context of the culture in which it originates.

deviation from ideal mental health: abnormality is seen as deviating from an ideal of positive mental health. Ideal mental health would include a positive attitude towards the self, resistance to stress and an accurate perception of reality.

deviation from social norms: abnormal behaviour is seen as a deviation from implicit rules about how one 'ought' to behave. Anything that violates these rules is considered abnormal.

eating disorder: a term that refers to a serious disruption of the eating habits or appetite and which may reflect abnormal psychological functioning. The most common eating disorders are anorexia nervosa and bulimia nervosa.

failure to function adequately: by using practical criteria of adequate functioning, mentally healthy people are judged as being able to operate within certain acceptable limits. If abnormal behaviour interferes with daily functioning, it might, according to these criteria, be considered abnormal.

statistical infrequency: abnormality is defined as those behaviours that are extremely rare, i.e. any behaviour that is statistically infrequent is regarded as abnormal.

Questions
&
Answers

In this section of the guide there are eight questions — four on Physiological Psychology and four on Individual Differences. Each question is worth 30 marks. You should allow 30 minutes when attempting to answer a question, dividing that time according to the mark allocation for each part. The section is structured as follows:

- sample questions in the style of the unit
- example candidate responses at the B- or C-grade level (candidate A) — these demonstrate both strengths and weaknesses of responses with potential for improvement
- example candidate responses at the A-grade level (candidate B) — such answers demonstrate thorough knowledge, a good understanding and an ability to deal with the data that are presented in the questions

Examiner's comments

All candidate responses are followed by examiner's comments. These are preceded by the icon *e*. They indicate where credit is due. In the weaker answers, they also point out areas for improvement, specific problems and common errors such as poor time management, lack of clarity, weak or non-existent development, irrelevance, misinterpretation of the question and mistaken meanings of terms.

The comments also indicate how each example answer would have been marked in an actual exam, using the criteria listed on pages 6–7.

Physiological psychology (I)

(a) What is meant by the terms 'stressor', 'immune system' and 'life changes'? (2+2+2 marks)

(b) Outline *two* physical methods for managing the negative effects of stress. (3+3 marks)

(c) Consider the view that stress plays an important role in the development of cardiovascular disorders. (18 marks)

Total: 30 marks

(a) Try to be concise when answering this type of question. If you are struggling to get your meaning across succinctly, try adding an example to show the examiner that you know what you are talking about. A sentence or two will normally suffice for such definitions. Check your understanding of these terms against the definitions provided on page 22.

(b) The key term here is 'outline'. Your textbooks will have extended descriptions of a variety of methods for managing the negative effects of stress (e.g. drugs, biofeedback). You must choose two and distil those down into a précis that can be written in a maximum of 3 minutes. It is important that any methods chosen are *physical* (e.g. drugs) rather than *psychological* (e.g. meditation). The question asks for *two* methods, so writing about more than two is a waste of time.

(c) This part of the question constitutes the AO1 + AO2 component, so it is important to treat it differently from the other parts. You are asked to 'consider the view that stress plays an important role in the development of cardiovascular disorders'. Does it? How do you know that? What evidence is there that stress plays such a role? Your answer should rise above merely *describing* evidence or documenting theoretical links between stress and cardiovascular disorders. It should construct a convincing case for such a link. You can, however, construct an argument that shows quite the opposite. Either approach is fine provided you are 'engaging' with the material in a logical and evaluative way. Try to reach a tentative conclusion such as 'Based on the results of research studies and from clinical evidence, it is evident that… However, it is also evident that stress is not the only cause of cardiovascular disorders, and the fact that many people who experience extreme stress *do not* develop such disorders suggests that…'.

■ ■ ■

Answer to question 1: candidate A

(a) A stressor is something that causes you stress, such as loud noise or an argument.
The immune system is the body's way of dealing with infection.
Life changes are major changes in your life, such as divorce.

Each of these answers is partially correct and is awarded 1 out of 2 marks. A stressor is some feature of the environment that activates the body's stress response systems. The second answer should have given some specific ways in which the immune system deals with infection. When used in this context, life changes are stressful events that involve major transitions or adaptations. (3 out of 6 marks)

(b) One physical method for managing stress is the use of drugs. These are known as anxiolytics because they reduce stress.

Biofeedback involves the person learning to control the physiological responses that are experienced as stress.

e Each of these answers is generally accurate but lacking detail and loses 1 mark. The first would be better if it included information about how drugs might reduce stress. The second should have included some detail about how biofeedback actually works. (4 out of 6 marks)

(c) Stress has long been thought to contribute to the development of cardiovascular disorders. Studies in the 1950s, 60s and 70s have shown that people in high-stress occupations are more prone to coronary disease than people in lower-stress occupations. In one study by Buell and Breslow (1960), workers who worked in industrial jobs for more than 48 hours a week were twice as likely to die of coronary heart disease than workers who worked less than 48 hours a week.

Although these studies appear to show that cardiovascular disorders, such as coronary heart disease, are caused by exposure to stress, it is not always clear from these studies whether the stress was the cause of the disease or a consequence of it. Research suggests that stress does not automatically produce cardiovascular disorders but that individuals have differing susceptibility to stress-related disorders. Friedman (1974) claimed that the Type A personality was prone to cardiovascular disorders whereas the Type B personality was more immune to the effects of stress and therefore less likely to develop cardiovascular disorders as a result of prolonged exposure to stressful situations.

e This is a well-informed answer which uses material clearly relevant to the question. It is accurate and offers the occasional insightful critical point. The Buell and Breslow research is presumably being offered to support the opening statement. We are told nothing else about this study or its conclusions, therefore we must conclude that stress and long hours are synonymous. There is no mention of the other work-related factors that might mediate in this relationship (such as the demands of the job, degree of control and so on). Long hours, we must conclude, lead to coronary heart disease. There is a good opening to the first paragraph, but we are taken no further in this argument (this is, after all, a reasonably short answer). The rest of the answer works with the material in a more effective manner, and examines the role of individual differences in vulnerability to cardiovascular disorders, although there is still a tendency to resort to descriptive material (i.e. AO1) rather than analytic/evaluative (i.e. AO2) material. Overall, the answer is reasonable in the amount of relevant content presented, limited in the level of commentary, and reasonably effective in the way that material is used. (AO1 — 3 out of 6 marks, AO2 — 5 out of 12 marks)

Total for this question: 15 out of 30 marks

Answer to question 1: candidate B

e The following answer is supported by material presented earlier in this book and is equivalent to a good grade-A response to this question.

(a) Stressors are events that cause a stress reaction in the body. They include environmental stressors such as workplace stressors or examinations, and life events such as divorce or bereavement.

The immune system is a system of cells within the body that is concerned with fighting against intruders such as viruses and bacteria. White blood cells (leucocytes) identify and kill foreign bodies (called antigens).

Life changes are events (such as divorce or bereavement) that necessitate a significant adjustment in various aspects of a person's life. As such, they can be seen as significant sources of stress in a person's life.

(b) One physical method for managing the negative effects of stress is the use of drugs. Benzodiazepine (BZ) anti-anxiety drugs work by reducing the activity of the neurotransmitter serotonin. Beta-blockers work by reducing activity in the pathways of the sympathetic nervous system and are therefore effective against raised heart rate and blood pressure.

Biofeedback is a technique for controlling physiological responses through receiving information about the body's stress response as it occurs. Monitoring devices provide the person with feedback whenever they change the response in the desired direction. The aim of this technique is to find a strategy to reduce a particular stress-related response which can then be transferred to the outside world and used regularly to relieve stress.

(c) Psychological research has demonstrated that stress can adversely affect the cardiovascular system. For example, Russek's (1962) study suggested a relationship between work stress and the development of coronary heart disease. Studies such as this suggest that work has only a negative effect on health, yet this is not the case. Some work characteristics can also be beneficial to health, in particular, energy expenditure. Research studies (e.g. Paffenbarger et al., 1984) have suggested that high energy expenditure at work might be associated with reduced risk of fatal heart attacks.

Karasek (1979) claimed that work characteristics can combine interactively in relation to health. A sample of Swedish working men was examined for depression, cardiovascular disease and mortality. Those workers whose jobs were characterised by heavy workloads combined with little latitude for decision-making fared worst. However, this ignores the moderating effect of social support on this relationship. Social support seems to play an essential role in the management of stress at work and serves as a buffer against possible adverse health effects of excessive psychological demands.

Friedman and Rosenman (1974) described Type A behaviour as a major behavioural risk factor for cardiovascular ill health. Different characteristics mark out the Type A individual whose risk of coronary heart disease is greatest. The issue of

question

control, for example, is an important one and may distinguish between the vulner-ability of Type As and the resistance of 'hardy' types (Kobasa, 1979). Kobasa's hardy types report feeling in control of their work and their lives. Type A behaviour predicts cardiovascular ill health, while hardiness predicts general good health.

The experience of stress, therefore, does not inevitably contribute to the development of cardiovascular disorders. For some, however, stress might adversely affect health. At the same time, however, a state of ill health can act as a significant source of stress, reducing an individual's ability to cope with other sources of stress. Within these limits, the assumption of a relationship between the experience of stress and poor health appears justified.

Question 2

Physiological psychology (II)

(a) What is meant by the terms 'workplace stressor', 'cardiovascular disorders' and 'psychological approach to stress management'?   (2+2+2 marks)

(b) Describe the procedures and findings of *one* study that has investigated the role of workplace stressors as a source of stress.   (6 marks)

(c) To what extent have psychological approaches been shown to be effective methods of stress management?   (18 marks)

Total: 30 marks

(a) Each of these three terms should be defined succinctly, perhaps also including an example to give extra clarity to the answer. You do not need to give long, detailed responses.

(b) Don't waste time writing about other aspects of your chosen study that are not asked for here (i.e. the aims or conclusions). The use of plurals in the question suggests that there is more than one 'procedure' and more than one 'finding'. This shouldn't worry you too much as the reporting of studies inevitably 'pluralises' things in this way. Although you need to include both procedures and findings to get into the top mark band, these don't have to be in the same detail or depth.

(c) The 'to what extent' instruction tells you that you should take a critical look at the effectiveness of psychological approaches to stress management. This can be achieved in a number of ways (e.g. through a consideration of the effectiveness of specific approaches, a comparison with physical approaches, or perhaps through a consideration of the mediating factors, such as individual differences or social support. The question does ask about the 'effectiveness' of such approaches (i.e. do they work?) rather than more general advantages and disadvantages, so your discussion should be guided by that requirement. Don't try to include every relevant point in your answer — high marks are given for answers that are informed and thorough. Be selective, and use material effectively.

■ ■ ■

Answer to question 2: candidate A

(a) A workplace stressor is something in the workplace (such as having to complete a job under time pressure) that causes a stress reaction in the worker.

Cardiovascular disorders are heart attacks and other, similar disorders that might be caused by stress.

The psychological approach to stress management involves dealing with stress with psychological methods (such as meditation) rather than taking drugs to lessen its effects.

The first answer is accurate and detailed, for 2 marks, and cleverly uses an example to add extra clarity to the answer. The second part is partially accurate for 1 mark. Cardiovascular disorders are more than just heart attacks, and adding that they might be caused by stress doesn't really make the answer much clearer. The last answer appears somewhat circular ('the psychological approach involves dealing with stress with psychological methods...') but it does add an example (meditation) and contrasts psychological methods directly with physical methods. This is accurate and detailed and deserves full marks. (5 out of 6 marks)

(b) One study that investigated the role of workplace stressors was carried out in a sawmill in Sweden by Johansson et al. They found that people who had very stressful jobs (those who were at the end of the manufacturing process) were more likely to experience stress than those further down the line. This is because the speed they worked at determined what everybody else in the factory was paid. The researchers found that this group of people took more days off work, due to sickness, and also showed more signs of stress when they were in work.

> There are two requirements in this question, to describe the procedures and the findings of an appropriate study. This very clearly does the latter, but apart from a brief mention of the location of the study, tells us nothing about how the researchers carried it out. It isn't necessary to describe both in the same detail, but they both have to be addressed to get the top marks. The findings are accurate and detailed, but the procedures are missing. (4 out of 6 marks)

(c) Psychological approaches to stress management, such as meditation and relaxation, have been shown to be very effective. It is not always convenient to practise these techniques, however, and they do little to deal with the effects of severe or long-term stress (such as a difficult job or looking after a relative who has a severe mental disorder). Other psychological techniques are more effective in these situations, and these include stress inoculation training. This technique is effective because it deals cognitively with the source of the stress, the ways that a person has dealt with this in the past and the way that they might deal with similar stressors in the future. Although this can be very effective, it does take a lot of time and requires a lot of commitment from the stressed person if it is to work.

If psychological approaches to stress management don't work, there are other, physical, approaches that are also very effective. The use of drugs such as BZs reduces the activity of the sympathetic nervous system and so makes the person less anxious. Drugs have the problem of leading to dependency and even addiction and so should only be used for short periods of time. Drugs only treat the symptoms rather than the causes of stress, so are not particularly effective.

> This answer starts very well, and focuses itself clearly on the question set (i.e. the effectiveness of psychological approaches to stress management). We are told that meditation and relaxation 'have been shown to be effective', but are not given any evidence to support this claim. We are told that this effectiveness might be dampened by the limitations of these techniques (a good point to make). Stress inoculation is treated in pretty much the same way, i.e. 'effective but...'. The second paragraph introduces the alternative approach (i.e. physical methods) but

this is not used as critical commentary on the psychological approach, so it is a bit of a mystery why it is included here. The answer has, after a good start, lost its way a little. Overall, its content is reasonable, the level of detail limited and the material is used reasonably effectively. (AO1 — 2 out of 6 marks, AO2 — 5 out of 12 marks)

Total for this question: 16 out of 30 marks

Answer to question 2: candidate B

✐ The following answer is supported by material presented earlier in this book and is equivalent to a good grade-A response to this question.

(a) A workplace stressor is some aspect of our working environment (such as work overload, impending deadlines or role ambiguity) that we experience as stressful and which causes a stress reaction in our body.

Cardiovascular disorders are disorders relating to the heart and blood vessels. These can be evident in physical damage to the blood supply system, which may in turn lead to the gradual blocking of a blood vessel (atherosclerosis).

The psychological approach to stress management involves the use of techniques (such as relaxation or specific cognitive–behavioural techniques) that are designed to help people cope better with stressful situations or to alter their perception of the demands of a stressful situation.

(b) Johansson et al. (1978) studied the 'finishers' in a timber mill — men who were responsible for the final stages of the timber preparation process and as such were responsible for the overall productivity of the workforce. The researchers measured levels of stress hormones during work days and rest days, and took other measurements such as sickness and absenteeism.

These workers had raised levels of stress hormones on work days and a higher incidence of stress-related health problems than other workers in the process. They also showed higher levels of absenteeism than other workers at the sawmill.

(c) Psychological approaches to stress can either be general, such as using relaxation techniques or meditation to reduce the body's state of arousal, or specific, using cognitive and behavioural training. Although relaxation techniques can be useful by reducing the levels of stress response, their action is non-specific. Effective long-term stress reduction requires intervention focused on the source of the stress. As with relaxation techniques, the action of meditation techniques is non-specific rather than focused on effective intervention at source.

The concept of 'hardiness' (Kobasa and Maddi, 1977) is taken to mean resistance to illness or ability to deal with stress. Kobasa proposed that hardiness could be improved, with people encouraged to take on challenges that they can cope with, thus reinforcing feelings of control. Studies have supported the claim that increasing hardiness is an effective method of stress management. Hardy types have been shown to be less vulnerable to cardiovascular disorders in stressful situations than those who display Type A behaviour because of the increased control they believe they have over their lives. However, Kobasa's studies have tended to involve middle-class businessmen, therefore the results cannot reliably be generalised to other social and cultural groups.

Meichenbaum's stress-inoculation model focuses on both the nature of the stress problem and the ways of coping with stress. This combination of cognitive strategies and behavioural techniques makes stress-inoculation a potentially effective way of managing stress. Despite this potential, however, few controlled studies have confirmed its predictions.

The effectiveness of any particular approach to stress management is also affected by other factors that mediate in its influence. For example, some people try to protect themselves from the full impact of a stressful situation by denying, playing down, or emotionally detaching themselves from it. Providing information to these people (as in the cognitive approaches) can actually increase their stress levels, rather than decrease them. Response to stress can also be eased by support from either the family or the community. For example, studies have shown that women who have close, confiding relationships are better able to deal with potentially stressful situations and are less likely to develop stress-related psychiatric disorders.

Physiological psychology (III)

(a) Give *two* differences between the physical and psychological approach to
stress management. (3 + 3 marks)
(b) Outline research into life changes as sources of stress. (6 marks)
(c) 'The impact of stress is, in part, determined by the culture in which one lives.'
To what extent are the effects of stress modified by cultural factors? (18 marks)

Total: 30 marks

(a) Questions such as this do take a little thinking about, as you cannot simply
regurgitate an answer learned previously. The essential differences between the
two approaches are: physical approaches such as drugs tend to change the body's
reaction to stress, and deal specifically with the physical symptoms of stress;
psychological methods tend more to teach us how to minimise the negative impact
of stress and teach positive coping responses.

(b) This question isn't asking you to give details of one specific study (although that
is one way of answering the question), but to outline research in general in this
area. This might include the methods used in such research (such as the social
readjustment rating scale or SRRS) or the findings/conclusions of individual studies.
Take care, however, to restrict your answer to 'life events' as sources of stress
(rather than other contributory sources), and keep your account descriptive
(i.e. don't include evaluation — it isn't asked for here).

(c) As with all the AO1 + AO2 questions you will encounter, this one requires more
than just a straightforward description of the relationship between stress and
cultural factors. There will be some descriptive material but, as always, it is what
you do with that material that is all important here. For example, we might assume
that there are cultural differences in the way that people experience and deal with
stress, but is this the case? Does research support this claim, and what problems
might we encounter when determining this relationship? You could also focus on
any conclusions that might be evident from this relationship between culture and
stress, for example the increased nature of social support that might be the norm
in collectivist societies.

■ ■ ■ ◢

Answer to question 3: candidate A

(a) Psychological approaches involve relaxation whereas physical approaches just
involve giving someone a drug to make things better.
Psychological approaches teach people how they can deal more effectively with
stressful situations whereas physical approaches just deal with the symptoms.

The first answer is basic and worth just 1 mark. Psychological approaches to stress
management involve far more than just relaxation, and physical approaches involve

more than simply administering drugs. There is little detail here other than a simple acknowledgement of an example drawn from each approach. There is no real attempt to differentiate between the two approaches, either globally or specifically (using the examples given here). The second answer is a decent, if limited, attempt to detail a difference between the two approaches. Psychological approaches do help people to deal more effectively with stressful situations, and by focusing on the body's physiological response to stress, physical methods might be said to be addressing only the symptoms. More detail is needed here, but this is worth 2 marks. (3 out of 6 marks)

(b) Holmes and Rahe developed a scale that measured the impact of life events on stress and the development of stress-related disorders. The SRRS measured the levels of stress that people had experienced over the previous 2 years. Holmes and Rahe found that those people who had experienced a number of major life changes (such as the death of a spouse or divorce) were more likely to show stress-related illnesses. A problem with measures such as the SRRS is that the data are only correlational, so do not tell us whether one thing (such as the divorce) has caused the other (the illness). Another problem is that people enter a 'search for meaning' and might try to explain their current depression by reporting more negative life events over the previous 2 years.

    This is an accurate account of Holmes and Rahe's work using the SRRS. It includes a couple of criticisms of the use of the scale as a research tool which, although not asked for in the question, receive some credit here as they add information that is important when interpreting the results of such research. We are told that the SRRS produces a correlational analysis between life events and stress-related illnesses, and also (possibly the result of different research) that people who have experienced a significant negative life event tend to recall more negative life events in the previous 2 years. This is accurate and detailed, but perhaps closer to the criteria of the band below. (5 out of 6 marks)

(c) Research has shown that different cultural groups cope with stress in different ways. For example, the existence of social support networks, a characteristic of African-Americans, modifies the effects of stress for members of these groups. In one study, it was found that, among the carers of Alzheimer's patients, African-Americans expressed different attitudes towards their role. They were also more likely, compared with White Americans, to use their religion as support, and this appeared to lower their feelings of stress.

    Research has suggested that the effects of stress are modified by the culture in which a person lives. However, it is not always that easy to disentangle all the ways in which cultures differ in order to find out which of these characteristics is most responsible for minimising the effects of stress. Cultures differ in many ways, for instance, what people eat, how they live and what sort of jobs they do. Each of these could contribute to the experience of stress, but it is very difficult to determine exactly how and why they do. There are also differences between cultures in whether people feel they should be stressed. Cynics believe that stress is a Western phenomenon, and in other parts of the world people just get on with things and are less likely to go to a doctor complaining about stress. This might mean that we get a rather disjointed view of the true extent of stress and how people cope with it.

e There is some very good material here, although it is not always used as effectively as it might have been. There is an opening claim that different cultural groups cope with stress in different ways, and this claim is supported by the study of the carers of Alzheimer's patients. We are then told that it is difficult to establish which actual difference between cultures is responsible for differences in coping with stress. This is another good point, although more might have been made of it. The answer ends with the claim that stressors might be the same in all cultures, but people's attitudes to them differ. This is an appropriate point to make, and deserves credit. Overall, this has a reasonable amount of relevant material, with a limited level of analysis, but the material is used effectively. (AO1 — 4 out of 6 marks, AO2 — 7 out of 12 marks)

Total for this question: 19 out of 30 marks

■ ■ ■

Answer to question 3: candidate B

e The following answer is supported by material presented earlier in this book and is equivalent to a good grade-A response to this question.

(a) Physical approaches to stress management affect the bodily systems associated with stress (for example through the use of drugs that change the way the body reacts to stress). Psychological approaches attempt to reduce the arousal associated with stress in other ways such as through relaxation or meditation.

Physical approaches to stress management might simply suppress the physical symptoms of stress, whereas psychological approaches might involve the development of active coping strategies or a reappraisal of the stressful situation itself.

(b) Holmes and Rahe developed the social readjustment rating scale (SRRS) to explore the relationship between stress-related disorders and experience of stressful life events. Each of 43 life events (such as divorce or bereavement) was rated for the impact it might have on a person. The researchers then asked people to indicate which of these life events they had experienced over the previous 2 years. Their total score was used as an indication of the stress in that person's life. Holmes and Rahe discovered that the higher the score on the SRRS, the more likely people were to be suffering from a stress-related health problem.

Rather than focusing on life events, which are fairly unusual, other research (e.g. Kanner et al., 1981) has investigated the role of daily hassles (negative everyday events) and uplifts (positive everyday events) in mental health. This has demonstrated a positive correlation between daily hassles and levels of depression, anxiety and other health problems. However, research tends not to support any proposed relationship between uplifts and our health status.

question

(c) Social support appears to be one of the most important factors that protect people against the negative effects of stress. Kim and McKenry (1998) found strong cultural differences in the degree to which members of different cultures relied on family or other close relationships for social support. For example, Asian and other collectivist cultures tend to emphasise interdependence among individuals. By contrast, North American and other individualist cultures tend to emphasise independence. These differences illustrate how culturally defined differences can influence the interpretation of stressful events, the resources that individuals bring to bear under stress and hence the effectiveness of their attempts to cope.

Research has tended to support the claim that cultural differences alter the impact of stress for individuals. Leong and Mallinckrodt (1990) found that White American students reported significantly more chronic stress-related physical symptoms than did Asian American students, and also reported greater concerns about drug and alcohol use problems (an indication of their reaction to greater life stresses). Research has also demonstrated the important distinction between 'received support' (the amount or frequency of actual support received) and 'perceived support' (the person's perception that support is available if needed). Many findings suggest that perceived support (a characteristic of collectivist cultures) is extremely important in alleviating the psychological and physical distress associated with stress, perhaps even more so than the actual level of support received.

Because of the difficulties of making direct comparisons across cultures, it is hard to disentangle the effects of stress and stress management from other factors that might affect the impact of stress or the effectiveness of a coping response. Research by Weg (1983), for example, among the Abkarsian people of Georgia, found that their longevity was the result of a combination of factors. These included genetic inheritance, strong social support, physically active lifestyle, no alcohol or smoking and low reported stress levels.

Physiological psychology (IV)

(a) Outline the *three* stages of general adaptation syndrome. (2+2+2 marks)

(b) Describe the procedures and conclusions of one study of the relationship between stress and illness. (6 marks)

(c) 'The use of physical strategies, such as drugs or biofeedback, may soften the impact of stress, but does little to help us deal effectively with its potentially negative effects.'

Outline and evaluate the physical approach to stress management. (18 marks)

Total: 30 marks

(a) One can do little more in the time available than define each of the stages of GAS. This shouldn't be too difficult, but don't spend too much time outlining one stage to the detriment of the others. Two minutes of writing and thinking time should produce about 25–30 words, which is easily enough for outlining each stage.

(b) As with all questions that ask for specific aspects of a study, this should be approached carefully. The question does *not* ask for the aims or the findings, so don't waste time putting these in as well. Describing 'procedures' requires details of how the researchers organised the study and how they collected their data. Describing 'conclusions' requires more than a simple statement of the main findings. For example, a research study might have *found* that 70% of hospital doctors who work in excess of 50 hours a week show signs of cardiovascular disorders. The conclusion, on the other hand, might be that people exposed to significant work-related stress over long periods of time are more vulnerable to stress-related illness.

(c) There is some clear guidance in the quotation that accompanies this question, so you should be off to a flying start. Try to avoid the temptation to describe only physical approaches to stress management (such as drugs and biofeedback). You are also being asked to *evaluate* them here. If you are going to mention psychological approaches, this should be only as part of a critical appraisal of the alternative physical approaches. It is not sufficient simply to add a mention of *psychological* approaches in the vain hope that it will get you a few extra marks. Remember that one of the key criteria for AO2 marks is how *effectively* the material has been used.

■ ■ ■

Answer to question 4: candidate A

(a) The alarm stage is when the presence of a stressor causes the activation of the body's stress response, preparing the body to react to the potential threat from the stressor.

The resistance stage is when the body's stress response copes with the stressful situation and the body tries to return to normal — body temperature and blood pressure return to normal.

The exhaustion stage is when the body can no longer cope with the stressful situation — it is exhausted.

Accurate and detailed accounts are provided for the first two stages (2 out of 2 marks for each). The outline of the third stage is fairly basic — it is the body's resources and its defence against the stressor that are exhausted. The individual becomes more vulnerable to stress-related disorders at this point. This loses 1 mark. (5 out of 6 marks)

(b) Cohen et al. (1993) studied men and women in order to see if the level of stress in their lives could in any way affect their susceptibility to illness. The aim of this study was to see if high levels of personal stress make people more vulnerable to infectious diseases.

In order to do this, the researchers measured the stress that each person was under, and then exposed them to a variety of infections (such as the cold virus).

They found that people high in personal stress were more likely to catch the infections, showing that high levels of stress increase our susceptibility to infectious illnesses.

This answer has incorporated all the different aspects of this study (i.e. the aims, procedures, findings and conclusions). An examiner would need to pick through this to establish the procedures and conclusions (as required here). The third sentence ('In order to do this...') is credited as procedures, and the latter half of the final sentence ('...showing that high levels of stress...') is credited as the conclusions. There is a lesson to be learned here — be selective and stress the areas that are required; don't stick down everything and hope for the best. (3 out of 6 marks)

(c) The physical approach to stress management involves drugs such as Valium and the use of biofeedback. Drugs work by making the person less anxious about a situation, but can also have side effects. Drugs such as Valium can be addictive and even if they were not physically addictive, people may come to rely on them, and so become psychologically addicted to the relief that they bring. One of the main problems with the use of drugs to combat stress is that they can only help treat the symptoms. For example, drugs like beta-blockers lower blood pressure, but don't help the person cope with the stressful situation in any other way. That is why psychologists use psychological methods like stress-inoculation, because these teach the individual more effective strategies for overcoming stress.

Biofeedback involves giving someone a small electric shock to the side of the head to relieve them of the stress. This can be very effective, particularly if they are so stressed they are feeling suicidal. However, critics of biofeedback claim that it is equivalent to hitting a television set because it doesn't work. There are also side effects in using biofeedback, particularly as it can cause serious memory losses, and in some older patients it can actually kill them.

Other biological methods like alcohol or drugs of abuse might help the person to escape temporarily from the stressful situation, but can cause further problems of their own, as people become addicted to drugs or dependent on alcohol. This can cause problems with holding down a job or looking after a family, and this further contributes to the stress the person is under.

 The first paragraph of this answer includes quite a good evaluation of the problems of using drugs as a method of stress management. Drugs can become physically addictive and people may also develop psychological dependence on them. There is also the good point that drugs only treat the symptoms of stress, doing nothing to help people learn how to cope with stress. The second paragraph has mixed up biofeedback with electroconvulsive therapy (ECT) and therefore is evaluating completely the wrong type of treatment. A very sensible point is made in the final paragraph about the dangers of palliative strategies such as alcohol and drugs of abuse. Overall, ignoring the second paragraph, the answer offers a reasonable response to the question, although the level of analysis of the biological approach to stress management is limited. Material is used effectively, however. (AO1 — 2 out of 6 marks, AO2 — 7 out of 12 marks)

Total for this question: 17 out of 30 marks

Answer to question 4: candidate B

 The following answer is supported by material presented earlier in this book and is equivalent to a good grade-A response to this question.

(a) In the alarm stage, the sympathetic branch of the ANS is activated. This increases heart rate and blood pressure and the release of hormones that maintain and increase sympathetic activity.

In the resistance stage, the body attempts to cope with the stressor by maintaining the same level of arousal.

In the exhaustion stage, the body's resources and defences against the stressor become exhausted. At this stage, stress-related conditions such as ulcers and raised blood pressure can develop.

(b) Russek (1962) sent questionnaires to four groups of age-matched medical professionals. Two of these groups (GPs and anaesthetists) were judged to be highly stressed, and two (pathologists and dermatologists) were judged to be under low stress levels. The questionnaires measured family diet and incidence of coronary heart disease in the sample.

This study confirmed the relationship between stress associated with job responsibility and the development of coronary heart disease. Russek further concluded that such stress seemed to be far more significant than hereditary factors or a high-fat diet in the development of heart disease.

question

(c) The physical approach to stress management is characterised predominantly by the use of drugs and biofeedback. Anti-anxiety drugs such as the benzodiazepine (BZ) class of drug work by blocking the activity of the neurotransmitter serotonin. Beta-blockers work by reducing activity in the pathways of the sympathetic nervous system, and therefore are effective against raised heart rate and blood pressure. Research has shown that anti-anxiety drugs such as the BZs help to reduce the anxiety that might accompany stressful experiences. However, such drugs can be over-used and abused, and may themselves cause problems. Research evidence suggests that the long-term use of BZs can actually erode a person's ability to deal with stress, leading to greater dependence on the drug over time. Drugs are also limited because they only treat the symptoms of stress, not the causes. Most stressors are psychological, so physical measures do not address the real cause of the problem, nor can they be relied on for significant and lasting improvements.

Biofeedback is a technique for controlling physiological responses by receiving information about the body's stress response as it occurs. The aim of this technique is to find a strategy to reduce a particular stress-related response which can be used regularly to relieve stress in the outside world. Although it is claimed that biofeedback techniques can have significant positive effects in the reduction of generalised anxiety disorders, the use of this technique and the related efforts to reduce heart rate in sufferers of anxiety disorders have had only limited success. Research evaluating the effectiveness of biofeedback has also suggested that biofeedback might be no more effective than muscle relaxation in the absence of biofeedback. This is a critical issue as biofeedback can be expensive as a technique.

The effectiveness of the physical approach to stress management might also be determined by other, non-physical factors. For example, the impact of stressful events is affected by our social systems. Response to stress can be eased by support from either the family or the community. For example, studies have shown that women who have close, confiding relationships are less likely to develop stress-related psychiatric disorders, and are better able to deal effectively with them when they do develop.

question 5

Individual differences (I)

(a) What is meant by the terms 'cultural relativism', 'anorexia nervosa' and 'bulimia nervosa'? **(2+2+2 marks)**

(b) Explain anorexia nervosa from the perspective of *one* psychological model of abnormality. **(6 marks)**

(c) To what extent can eating disorders such as anorexia nervosa be explained from a biological perspective? **(18 marks)**

Total: 30 marks

(a) These are quite tricky terms to define. 'Cultural relativism' does not lend itself to easy and precise definition, and the two eating disorders defy simple terms to describe them. However, these are quite legitimate terms for this sort of question, so you need to acquire definitions that will serve this purpose. The terms on page 34 should help you.

(b) There are four important aspects of this question. (1) The question asks for an *explanation* (it does not require criticisms — they come in the next question). (2) It asks for an explanation of *anorexia nervosa* (so you need not mention bulimia nervosa). (3) It asks you to explain it from the perspective of a *psychological* model of abnormality (be sure you understand what this means). (4) It asks for *one* perspective, so don't waste time writing about more than one.

(c) Questions such as this invite you to engage in a critique of the topic in question. In this case you are required to determine the extent to which biological explanations of anorexia nervosa have been successful in explaining this disorder. This is not an invitation to present a descriptive account of these explanations, but rather an invitation to *evaluate* them. There is no limit to the number of biological explanations that might be used in this assessment, so you might draw your arguments from biochemistry, brain dysfunction or genetics. It is permissible to include some descriptive content — it is difficult, after all, to construct an evaluative response without ever describing what you are evaluating. However, you should use this only as the basis of your critical argument.

Answer to question 5: candidate A

(a) Cultural relativism means that different cultures have different ideas about abnormality.

Anorexia is an eating disorder that means that the sufferer fears becoming fat and so refuses to eat, becoming dangerously underweight as a result.

Bulimia is also an eating disorder and means binge-eating followed by vomiting.

The first definition loses 1 mark. It is partially accurate in that it demonstrates that what is 'abnormal' is relative to its cultural context. This would have been improved by adding that when classifying behaviour as abnormal we should consider its cultural context. There are several relevant points included in the second answer, which is awarded full marks. The third defintion loses 1 mark. Bulimia is an eating disorder and does involve the cycle of bingeing and vomiting, but there are other details (such as the obsession with weight or the fact that bulimics are closer to an acceptable body weight) that might have been included for the full 2 marks. (4 out of 6 marks)

(b) The behaviourist explanation explains anorexia in terms of the learning experiences that a person has. They may, for example, have been praised for losing weight (operant conditioning) or might associate being overweight with anxiety (classical conditioning). People are also exposed to thin models in the media, so might strive to be like them and think themselves abnormal if they are not.

 This is accurate and does include three different forms of learning experience that might lead to the development of anorexia nervosa. It does cry out for a little more development in each of these areas, so would be described as accurate but less detailed. Remember to make the most of the time available. A question worth 6 marks should produce an answer that is around the 100-word range. This is only 61 words. (4 out of 6 marks)

(c) Anorexia nervosa is characterised by a number of symptoms, including being grossly underweight and not being aware of it. Anorexics also have a fear of becoming fat and may see themselves as far fatter than they actually are. Another symptom of anorexia (in women) is a lack of periods.

A person suffering from bulimia nervosa alternates binge-eating and vomiting as they try to rid themselves of the extra weight they have put on during the binge phase. A person with bulimia may be closer to their normal weight.

There are biological and psychological explanations for anorexia. There is some evidence that people with an eating disorder might have something wrong with an area of the brain known as the hypothalamus. This is the on–off switch for eating. However, most of the research on this has been done on animals; human eating may be due more to social and psychological factors.

One of these is the influence of the media. People are constantly exposed to images of thin people in the media and convinced that it is good to be thin. Also, they are exposed to lots of dieting magazines and other products with the message that they can be thin. Anorexia can then develop as they diet excessively. Another psychological explanation is the behavioural explanation, which explains anorexia in terms of the reinforcement that people receive when they lose weight. Anorexia then develops from a habit that gets out of hand, and also because people feel good when they are thin, and so are more likely to repeat the experience.

There are many explanations of anorexia and bulimia nervosa, and it is clear that explaining these from only a biological perspective is inadequate.

 This answer begins, as do many such answers, with a description of the clinical characteristics of anorexia nervosa and bulimia nervosa. These are not asked for, but the question appears to have started a 'tape loop' which runs regardless of the specific requirements of the question. This first section would get no marks. There then follows a brief description of the role of the hypothalamus, together with a (brief) evaluation of this model when applied to humans. The major part of the answer is devoted to a description of alternative psychological explanations of anorexia nervosa. This is weak on a number of counts. First, it doesn't answer the question set. Second, it is mostly descriptive (although this does pick up AO1 marks). Third, although it uses alternative perspectives, there is no attempt to construct an argument that would justify their inclusion. The commentary is superficial, the analysis rudimentary and there is minimal interpretation of the material being offered. (AO1 — 2 out of 6 marks, AO2 — 3 out of 12 marks)

Total for this question: 13 out of 30 marks

■ ■ ■

Answer to question 5: candidate B

 The following answer is supported by material presented earlier in this book and is equivalent to a good grade-A response to this question.

(a) Cultural relativism is the view that behaviour cannot be judged properly unless it is viewed in the context of the culture in which it originates.

Anorexia nervosa is a type of eating disorder in which the person, despite being seriously underweight, fears that they might become obese and therefore engages in self-starvation to prevent this happening.

Bulimia nervosa is a type of eating disorder in which a person habitually engages in episodes of uncontrollable eating (known as bingeing) followed by self-induced vomiting or other compensatory behaviours. Bulimics have an abnormal concern with body size and a morbid fear of being or becoming fat.

(b) The behaviourist explanation of eating disorders sees dieting and the quest for thinness as a habit, with the individual associating thinness with the admiration of others or with feelings of positive well-being. As other people frequently provide reinforcement for the new 'thin' person, the refusal to eat becomes an effective way of gaining such 'rewards'. The media can also cause people to develop distorted views of what is a 'normal' body image. Through dieting and exercise a person may strive to achieve the 'idealised' body that they see modelled in the media. As body weight drops below a critical point, eating disorders such as anorexia nervosa can be triggered.

(c) Genetic explanations of eating disorders such as anorexia nervosa are supported by family and twin studies which have shown that there is an increased risk of eating disorders among first-degree relatives of individuals with an eating disorder than among the general population. For example, Strober et al. (2000) compared the incidence of anorexia nervosa and bulimia nervosa in genetic relatives of probands diagnosed with anorexia or bulimia, with relatives of matched comparison subjects without an eating disorder. They concluded that both anorexia nervosa and bulimia nervosa ran in families. Their cross-transmission in families suggests a common, or shared, familial vulnerability to these disorders. Holland et al. (1984) found a 55% concordance rate for MZ twins compared with only 7% for DZ twins.

However, although there are significantly higher concordance rates for MZ twins than for DZ twins, this still leaves a large percentage of twins where the 'other' twin of an affected individual does not develop an eating disorder (Prentice, 2000). Hsu (1990) suggests that the genetic element of eating disorders might relate more to personality traits, such as emotional instability, which make such individuals more susceptible to life events, and hence to eating disorders.

It is believed that the lateral hypothalamus and ventromedial hypothalamus work together to set up a 'weight thermostat' which maintains a set point for weight. It is possible that a malfunction in the hypothalamus might explain the development of eating disorders. Although the role of the hypothalamus in the eating behaviour of animals is well documented, there is little conclusive evidence that eating orders might be influenced in the same way in humans.

It is also not clear why some people manage to gain control over the compensatory mechanisms necessary to maintain the correct weight level, while others become caught in a cycle of bingeing and purging. It seems likely that the psychological differences between anorexia and bulimia sufferers are important in this respect.

Individual differences (II)

(a) Give *two* differences between anorexia nervosa and bulimia nervosa. (3 + 3 marks)
(b) Describe the procedures and findings of *one* research study that has
   investigated the biological origins of anorexia nervosa or bulimia nervosa. (6 marks)
(c) Consider the problems faced by psychologists in the definition of
   abnormality. (18 marks)

Total: 30 marks

(a) This is not an invitation simply to list characteristics of anorexia and bulimia, but an opportunity to show in what way these are clinically *different* disorders. There are a number of differences between these disorders (e.g. anorexics refuse or are unable to maintain a healthy body weight, whereas bulimics are closer to their normal body weight, and might even be overweight), but you are only required to give two here. There are 3 marks for each, so you should attempt to answer in appropriate detail for each one.

(b) As with all questions that ask for specific aspects of a research study, this one requires careful consideration about its exact requirements. First, it asks for the *procedures* (i.e. how they carried out the study) and *findings* (i.e. the main results of the study) of a research study of *either* anorexia or bulimia. It also specifies that this should be a research study that has investigated the *biological* origins of these disorders (e.g. the role of genetics, biochemical changes, hypothalamic dysfunction, etc.).

(c) Here is a great temptation simply to describe the different definitions of abnormality (deviation from social norms, failure to function adequately, etc.), but the question asks you to consider the ways in which such definitions might be problematic. There is no requirement to cover *all* the major definitions as given on page 34, although using a number of these does highlight the arbitrariness of the process. It is also appropriate to consider the problems of determining abnormality within a cultural context.

■ ■ ■

Answer to question 6: candidate A

(a) An anorexic refuses to eat, so cannot maintain a healthy body weight. They tend to be dangerously underweight as a result. In bulimia, however, the person may binge eat. They tend to be closer to their natural body weight than anorexics.

This is a tricky one to disentangle. There *are* two differences here, but we must tease them apart. We are told that an anorexic *refuses to eat* whereas a bulimic will *binge* eat. This is the first difference, but it is basic and lacking detail, for 1 mark. Other details would have extended this difference, such as *why* an anorexic refuses to eat, or the cycle of binge–vomit in the bulimic. The second difference appears to be concerned with body weight. We are told that the anorexic *cannot maintain a healthy body weight* and is *dangerously underweight*. On the other hand, the bulimic is *closer to their natural body weight*. This is generally accurate but not sufficiently detailed for 3 marks. (3 out of 6 marks)

(b) Holland et al. (1984) studied identical and non-identical twins and tested them to see if they had anorexia if the other twin was anorexic. They found that among identical twins there was a 1 in 2 chance that one twin would be anorexic if the other had the disorder. This figure was much lower among non-identical twins.

e First, both parts of the question are satisfied. The answer does cover procedures *and* findings. The procedures are a little on the superficial side, and the findings, although accurate, only tell us that the non-identical twins had a 'much lower' concordance rate (the actual figures in this research were 55% and 7% respectively). You do not need to present both aspects (i.e. procedures and findings) in equal depth, but the amount of detail that you give will obviously influence the mark awarded. The content is limited, generally accurate, but lacking in detail. (3 out of 6 marks)

(c) There are many different ways of defining abnormality and all have their problems. The deviation from social norms definition defines abnormality as any behaviour that is different from the norm, for example talking to oneself. One of the problems with this definition is that talking to oneself might be considered normal in some cultures.

The deviation from the statistical norm definition explains behaviour that is rare as being abnormal. But under this definition, exceptional musical talent would be seen as abnormal, when clearly it is not. This is a very important problem, as psychiatrists must decide which statistically infrequent behaviours are abnormal, and which are not.

One of the problems of definition of abnormality was highlighted by Rosenhan's work 'Being sane in insane places'. Rosenhan sent a number of 'pseudopatients' to a psychiatric outpatients department, where they claimed that they heard voices. They were diagnosed as suffering from schizophrenia, even though they showed no further symptoms during their stay in hospital. Rosenhan then told hospitals that he was going to send more pseudopatients and, over the next few months, many were discovered by psychiatrists, even though Rosenhan hadn't sent any! All this shows that it is difficult to define what is and what is not abnormal.

e The treatment of the first two definitions (deviation from social norms and deviation from the statistical norm) is generally accurate but not particularly detailed. The inclusion of Rosenhan's study is appropriate, but it is not used particularly effectively. There is a good deal of descriptive content for this study, with a fairly weak concluding sentence to put it into the context of the question. Overall, the answer is reasonable, if a little limited, although it is clearly more competent at a descriptive (AO1) level than at an evaluative (AO2) level. (AO1 — 4 out of 6 marks, AO2 — 3 out of 12 marks)

Total for this question: 13 out of 30 marks

■ ■ ■

Answer to question 6: candidate B

e The following answer is supported by material presented earlier in this book and is equivalent to a good grade-A response to this question.

(a) Anorexics generally deny any abnormal eating behaviour and are preoccupied with losing more and more weight. Bulimics, on the other hand, recognise that their eating pattern is abnormal, and seek to reach an ideal, though not necessarily realistic, weight.

Anorexics have a distorted body image and turn away from food as a way of coping with their problems. Though dissatisfied with their body shape or weight, bulimics have a generally more accurate body image.

(b) Strober et al. (2000) obtained rates of anorexia nervosa and bulimia nervosa from 1831 first-degree relatives of 504 probands on the basis of clinical interviews and family history. Estimates of diagnosis based on all available information were given without knowledge of proband status or the identity of the person being assessed.

Whereas anorexia nervosa was rare in families of the comparison subjects (those who did not have an eating disorder), the incidence of anorexia nervosa was higher in female relatives of both anorexic and bulimic probands. Bulimia nervosa was more common than anorexia nervosa in female relatives of comparison subjects, but it, too, was found mainly in the families of those who suffered from either anorexia or bulimia nervosa.

(c) The statistical infrequency definition defines any characteristic that is statistically rare as abnormal. However, some behaviours are statistically infrequent yet are not classified as 'abnormal'. Judging which behaviours are infrequent and abnormal (as opposed to infrequent and normal) must, therefore, involve some other criterion.

The 'deviation from social norms' approach defines abnormal behaviour as any behaviour that violates an implicit societal 'rule' concerning 'normal behaviour'. These rules reflect the moral standards of a particular culture. Therefore, under this definition, what is considered abnormal will differ from culture to culture. However, social norms change over time rather than being fixed and unchangeable. Attempts to diagnose abnormality in the UK might show evidence of 'cultural blindness'. The characteristics of the White population, it is claimed, are treated as normative and the behaviour of other racial or ethnic groups is interpreted as being indicative of some underlying abnormality.

People who are mentally healthy are typically seen as functioning within certain acceptable limits. Some apparently dysfunctional behaviour may, however, be

adaptive and functional for the individual. For example, panic attacks can ensure that the person receives previously unobtainable attention from others (the so-called 'neurotic paradox'). Some disorders are also more prevalent in women than in men, for example depression, yet this may be more a product of sociocultural (rather than individual) factors. By labelling this a 'mental disorder', clinicians are stigmatising the person rather than the sociocultural context that produced the depression.

The 'deviation from ideal mental health' definition focuses on the major criteria of positive mental health. If a person deviated from one or more of these criteria (such as having an accurate perception of reality), they would be vulnerable to a mental disorder. Most people, according to this definition, would fall short of ideal mental health, yet would not be considered to possess an 'abnormality'. Although it is possible to measure ideal physical health with reasonable objectivity, measuring ideal mental health with the same degree of objectivity is more difficult because the criteria are more vague.

uestion

7

Individual differences (III)

(a) Outline the 'statistical infrequency' and 'failure to function adequately' definitions of abnormality. (3 + 3 marks)

(b) Describe the cognitive model of abnormality in terms of its views on the causes of abnormality. (6 marks)

(c) Outline and evaluate attempts to explain the causes of anorexia nervosa. (18 marks)

Total: 30 marks

(a) Questions such as this are fairly predictable, but there is still room to slip up when answering them. First, you have only 3 minutes to describe each one (hence the *outline* instruction). Second, you should make sure that you have outlined the important points of each one before spending time addressing examples. Examples can help make descriptions more explicit, but shouldn't be used *instead* of precise descriptive detail.

(b) The answer to this question should refer to the person's use of irrational thought processes. You are only being asked to describe the cognitive model's view on the *causes* of abnormality, so don't include anything about the *treatment* of abnormal behaviour. Nor are you required to evaluate the model here, so don't waste time and effort offering criticisms of this perspective.

(c) It is important to read this question *very* carefully before launching into a knee-jerk response. First, it asks for *attempts* in the plural, so you are required to evaluate more than one (genetics, media influence, psychodynamic explanations, etc.). Second, the question is clear about its specific requirements, asking for an evaluation of attempts to explain the *causes* of this disorder (not its clinical characteristics). Finally, the question asks for an outline and evaluation of attempts to explain *anorexia nervosa* (i.e. *not* bulimia nervosa). As with other AO1 + AO2 questions, it is important to remember that your response should not be purely *descriptive*. You are also asked for *evaluation* of these explanations.

■ ■ ■

Answer to question 7: candidate A

(a) The statistical infrequency definition explains abnormality in terms of things that are uncommon. For example, musical genius is uncommon, and therefore would be described as abnormal under this definition.

The failure to function adequately definition means that a person cannot look after themselves adequately in the view of others, and therefore needs help. For example, they might not be able to keep themselves clean or hold down a job, so would be described as abnormal by others.

There is some accuracy in the first part of this answer, although it is not really clear what is meant by 'uncommon' in this context. Musical genius is uncommon but would *not* be described as abnormal as suggested here. This part is worth just 1 mark. The second part of the answer, though including the essence of a correct definition, is rather clumsily expressed. It might be described as generally accurate but less detailed, rather than accurate and detailed, and earns 2 marks. (3 out of 6 marks)

(b) The cognitive model explains abnormal behaviour in terms of faulty ways of thinking about the world. For example, we should not expect everyone to like us, so it is perfectly normal for us to sometimes come across people who don't like us. If we were anxious about the fact that some people didn't like us, this would be seen as abnormal because of the faulty thinking that led us to this point.

> An accurate opening sentence is followed by an appropriate example that is described in some detail. The answer is limited in scope and detail (of the cognitive model's stance on the causes of abnormal behaviour) but is certainly not basic or flawed. (3 out of 6 marks)

(c) There have been a number of attempts to explain the causes of anorexia nervosa. For example, it has been explained in terms of a problem with the hypothalamus, with certain parts of the hypothalamus that control eating not working properly. Another biological explanation is that anorexia is inherited from parents. Research studies have shown that people who have this disorder often have a history of anorexia in their family background.

Biological explanations are not the only ways of explaining anorexia. Sociologists would explain it by saying that models in the media tend to be slim and the media generally represent thin as attractive. Research has also shown that if people move from a culture where there are no active media portraying lots of thin models, to a culture where there are, they become vulnerable to anorexia in the new culture.

Because the media show a lot of dieting adverts, people are led to believe that they must lose weight in order to become attractive. This is reinforced by the attitudes of others when a person does lose weight. If someone loses a significant amount of weight, they might like the reaction of others (i.e. their behaviour is reinforced by others) and be more inclined to repeat the behaviour until they reach a dangerously thin state (thought to be less than 85% of their normal body weight).

Biological explanations can offer one type of explanation for anorexia, but media explanations are better because they take account of the fact that people are influenced by what they see on television and read in magazines, and therefore are likely to be guided in their behaviour by the media, rather than being guided by their biology.

> This answer is far too focused on description, and the candidate spends most of the time allotted to this question in a descriptive trawl through a variety of explanations of anorexia. There are certainly opportunities for evaluation in this answer. For example, it would have been easy to rephrase the sentence 'Research studies

have shown that...' with the more evaluative 'This view is supported by research studies which have shown that...'. There is a superficial attempt made to offer evaluation (e.g. 'media explanations are better because...'), but overall there is simply too little that is addressing the specific requirements of the AO2 component of this question. (AO1 — 5 out of 6 marks, AO2 — 3 out of 12 marks)

Total for this question: 14 out of 30 marks

■ ■ ■

Answer to question 7: candidate B

📝 The following answer is supported by material presented earlier in this book and is equivalent to a good grade-A response to this question.

(a) Most human characteristics (including personality traits and behaviour) fall within a normal distribution, with most people clustering around the middle of the distribution (i.e. the norm), and fewer and fewer towards the edges. Any characteristic that is statistically rare according to this distribution is considered abnormal.

People who are mentally healthy are typically seen as functioning within certain acceptable limits (e.g. being able to look after oneself, or being able to carry on normal social discourse). If a person's behaviour interferes with their ability to operate within those limits, then it might be classified as abnormal. Behaviour that is bizarre (such as having hallucinations) or inefficient (such as being unable to leave the house because of obsessions) or which might be considered unpredictable or incomprehensible to others, might be defined as abnormal.

(b) The cognitive model stresses the role of irrational thought processes as a basis for abnormal functioning. These include: maladaptive assumptions about ourselves (such as the belief that there is a 'perfect' solution to all life's problems); specific upsetting thoughts (fleeting thoughts and images that occur 'automatically' in our thought processes); and illogical thinking processes (such as 'selective perception', where we see only the negative features of an event, and 'magnification', where we exaggerate the importance of undesirable experiences).

(c) Genetic explanations of anorexia nervosa have been supported by family and twin studies which have shown that there is an increased risk of eating disorders among first-degree relatives of an anorexic than among the general population. However, although there are significantly higher concordance rates for anorexia in MZ twins compared with DZ twins, this still leaves a large percentage of twins where the 'other' twin of an affected individual does not develop anorexia (Prentice, 2000).

It is possible that a malfunction in the hypothalamus can result in the development of anorexia. However, although the role of the hypothalamus in the eating behaviour of animals is well documented, there is little conclusive evidence that eating orders might be influenced in the same way in humans. It is also not

question

clear why some people manage to gain control over the compensatory mechanisms necessary to maintain the correct weight level (and hence develop anorexia), while others become caught in a cycle of bingeing and purging (and hence develop bulimia).

Behaviourist explanations of anorexia nervosa, which stress the importance of reinforcement in weight loss, might help to explain gender differences in anorexia. The emphasis on appearance and the pressure to be thin (a characteristic of Western societies) is aimed more at women than men. This has resulted in women being more concerned with being thin, more inclined to diet, and therefore more vulnerable to anorexia.

Psychodynamic explanations tend to stress the role of disturbed parent–child relationships in the development of eating disorders. For example, Bruch (1974) claimed that an anorexic, lacking self-reliance as a result of earlier parental conflict, tries to exert some personal control over their lives by controlling their body size. As with many psychodynamic explanations, however, Bruch's views on the causes of eating disorders lack objectivity. It is possible that the conflicts commonly found between the anorexic and their family might be the consequence of an eating disorder rather than its cause.

question 8

Individual differences (IV)

(a) Outline the clinical characteristics of anorexia nervosa and bulimia nervosa. (3+3 marks)

(b) Outline the assumptions of any *two* psychological models of abnormality in terms of their views on the causes of abnormal behaviour. (3+3 marks)

(c) 'What is considered "normal" or "abnormal" cannot be understood without also considering the cultural context of the behaviour being evaluated.' Consider how attempts to define abnormality might be influenced by cultural differences. (18 marks)

Total: 30 marks

(a) This is actually quite a tricky requirement, because there are more clinical characteristics of each disorder than could be described in 3 minutes. Implicit in this question is the word 'some', so pick some examples of the clinical characteristics (i.e. what characteristics of a person or their behaviour would make a psychiatrist apply the clinical label 'anorexia nervosa' or 'bulimia nervosa'?). Don't try to list them all in note form, as this would affect your 'quality of written communication' mark.

(b) It is important to take care over the time that you spend on each of the two models that you choose. It is very difficult to 'outline' the assumptions of, for example, the psychoanalytic view of abnormality in just 3 minutes, so you must be very disciplined in your time management. Practise doing just that until you feel comfortable with the time constraints. With such a strict time limit, it is vital that you don't stray beyond the exact requirements of the question.

(c) 'Consider how attempts to define abnormality might be influenced by cultural differences' might not *appear* to invite critical commentary, but it is required in your response. Our perception of the universality of mental disorders such as schizophrenia, depression, eating disorders, etc. arises out of our reliance on classificatory systems such as DSM and ICD. Is it appropriate to see abnormality as universal, or are we blind to cultural differences when assigning labels of abnormality? Although the question implies differences *between* cultures, it is also appropriate to consider differences *within* cultures (such as gender differences, social class differences and so on).

■ ■ ■

Answer to question 8: candidate A

(a) Anorexia nervosa is a fear of getting fat. People who display anorexia tend to have a distorted view of their body size, and won't eat because they are convinced they are too fat.

Bulimia nervosa means eating lots of junk food and then being sick.

The first answer is a limited but generally accurate account of some of the clinical characteristics of anorexia, for 2 marks. We would not expect a complete list of the characteristics, but perhaps a little more than this for the full 3 marks. The second part of the answer is basic and lacking in detail, but does show some under-standing of the bingeing and purging that is a characteristic of bulimia nervosa, for 1 mark. (3 out of 6 marks)

(b) The psychoanalytic explanation of eating disorders explains them in terms of inappropriate parenting when the child is young. This might leave the child with psychological difficulties which it can only solve in later life by becoming anorexic or bulimic. This gives the adolescent some control over their life.

The behaviourist explanation sees all behaviour as being learned, either through classical or operant conditioning. Pavlov discovered that behaviours could be learned through association, and Skinner's work with rats discovered that behaviour that was reinforced (i.e. rewarded) would be more likely to be repeated in the future.

 The first part is not a particularly accurate or detailed account of this view of eating disorders. This answer, based around Bruch's theory of the causes of eating disorders, does, however, mention that they might be caused by 'inappropriate parenting' (although we are not told in what way it might be inappropriate). The answer also suggests that this leaves the child with 'psychological difficulties' and that through anorexia or bulimia they can exercise 'some control over their life'. This lacks clarity and detail, but has enough appropriate information for 2 marks. The second answer is accurate as far as it goes, but makes no mention at all of eating disorders! This is a shame because it would have been fairly easy to use these concepts to explain how, for example, an anorexic might be 'reinforced' for their 'thinness' or to associate such thinness with the approval of others. Still, knowledge of the underlying principles gets some credit (1 mark). (3 out of 6 marks)

(c) There are some types of abnormality that are specific to a particular culture. These are known as culture-bound syndromes. An example would be windigo, which is found in the American Indians. This leads them to believe they will be possessed by a giant man-eating monster. Western psychiatry struggles to explain these sorts of conditions, yet to the people who have them they are real, rather than imaginary.

Some people believe that eating disorders are also examples of culture-bound syndromes because they appear in the West, where there is an abundance of food and lots of media representations of thin people. It has been shown that eating disorders are rare in non-Western cultures, but when people from those cultures move to the West, they become more vulnerable to eating disorders.

 This is a fairly competent, if short, response to the question. It does tend to be overly descriptive at the beginning, but makes good use of the material in the latter half of the answer. Rather than describing only culture-bound syndromes, it would have been more profitable to have considered the problems that these create for definitions of abnormality, and then use this information to construct a more searching response to the question set. There is certainly a commendable attempt to do just that at times, but in a far too limited way. The commentary would be described as superficial and the level of analysis as rudimentary, although the material is used reasonably effectively. (AO1 — 3 out of 6 marks, AO2 — 3 out of 12 marks)

Total for this question: 12 out of 30 marks

■ ■ ■

Answer to question 8: candidate B

e The following answer is supported by material presented earlier in this book and is equivalent to a good grade-A response to this question.

(a) Anorexics show a refusal to maintain normal body weight for their age and height, having a body weight of less than 85% of that expected. They have an intense fear of becoming fat, showing a disturbance in the way that their body weight or shape is experienced and a denial of the seriousness of their current low body weight. In post-menarchal girls, three consecutive menstrual cycles are absent.

Bulimics show recurrent episodes of binge-eating and inappropriate compensatory behaviours to prevent weight gain. These behaviours occur on average at least twice a week for a period of 3 months or more. A bulimic's self-evaluation is unduly influenced by body shape and weight.

(b) Psychoanalysis sees abnormal behaviour as being caused by underlying psychological forces, originating from childhood experiences or an unresolved conflict between id and superego. Because the immature ego is unable to deal with them at the time, disturbing experiences in childhood may be repressed and eventually re-emerge as psychological problems. Similarly, if the conflict between id and superego is not managed effectively by the ego, the person may develop a psychological disorder.

The behavioural model sees abnormality as the development of maladaptive behaviour patterns established through the principles of learning. Classical conditioning explanations of abnormal behaviour stress the maladaptive associations that are learned between two stimuli. Operant conditioning explanations stress the role of reinforcement in abnormal behaviour. Modelling stresses exposure to abnormal behaviours in significant others.

(c) Socio-cultural criteria for determining abnormality focus on whether the individual has internalised the views of their society. If an individual displays a behaviour that is outside society's expectations for appropriate behaviour, that behaviour is deemed as abnormal. The consequence of defining abnormality in this way is that, although a person might be considered abnormal in one culture, they might function better in another. Homosexuality, which was, until fairly recently, classified as a form of abnormality in America, was praised and seen as a means to a good life in many ancient cultures. In some Native American Indian tribes this practice was also accepted and honoured.

Just as society is in continual change, so too are the concepts of normality and abnormality. According to Freud, normality is a value-based concept. As a society, we decide who is normal and who is deviant, so normality is highly culture-specific. Defining abnormality in this way can be problematic, as any type of behaviour can be considered deviant by a culture at some point or another, a position known as cultural relativism. According to Gelfand et al. (1997), nearly all cultures identify some behaviours as abnormal.

Because the main classificatory systems for the assessment of abnormality are Western, it is not uncommon for Western psychiatrists mistakenly to identify as abnormal a behavioural pattern that is normal for a particular group. For example, it is considered normal for the Native American Indians to hear the voice of their recently deceased relatives talking to them, calling them from 'beyond the grave'. Cochrane and Sashidharan (1995) suggest that psychiatric diagnosis in the UK is 'culturally blind', with the behaviours of the White population being treated as normative. Any deviation from this is seen as indicative of an underlying pathology.

Within cultures, sub-groups can likewise differ in their experience of mental disorders. Women are more often diagnosed as suffering from depression and anxiety disorders than are men. However, this may reflect more the differences in male and female socialisation (including attitudes towards seeking help) than real differences between the sexes. Members of socially disadvantaged groups are more likely to be diagnosed with a major mental disorder. This might be a product of their more stressful life experiences, or a consequence of social drift, where the early onset of a mental disorder causes a downward spiral in the person's life chances. Social class then becomes a consequence of, rather than a contributory factor in, the diagnosis of a mental disorder.